FOREWORD

*H*ere is a book written by a very experienced music-lover for the encouragement of newcomers to the wonderful world of classical music.

In his Introduction the author has made a convincing case for writing the book; how successful has he been? He had first of all to decide whether to write a 'flip-through' guide to a large selection from a great number of composers, or to write at some length about a carefully considered few; choosing the latter course, he lays himself open to gentle criticism of his choice. There can be little argument about that precious handful of giants in the arts and, for the rest, personal judgement is paramount. Ian Christians emerges as a man of strong opinions, and some musicians might have frustration with his choice, but in the Introduction he explains his plan lucidly and convincingly.

His 'potted' biographies are just the thing for new listeners who will not want to be put off by too much specialised jargon, and bearing in mind that he aims to present his subjects as 'human', they are done with taste. He rightly stresses that the music he writes about is easily accessible to newcomers and he does his best to blow away the mists of snobbery and elitism which unfairly surround classical music.

I find that each composer is given a well-selected list from his works so that an enquiring mind may know where to start and continue a search for experience in listening to classical music for the first time; with such an ocean of material to choose from, many people are bewildered and discouraged from dipping a toe in the water.

Ian Christians is particularly to be congratulated for his comments on the unique and special experience of participating in music through attending concerts and operas. Bravo! say I, because if there is going to be this great explosion into listening to classical music, let it fill our concert halls and opera houses.

I enjoyed reading this book and I recommend it whole-heartedly to new music lovers everywhere.

Charles Groves

July 1991

The Author

Ian Christians is 47 and an experienced businessman who has been closely involved with the music industry on many fronts. A passionate believer in broadening the interest in classical music, he opened his first classical music (and wine) shop, Orpheus & Bacchus, in Guildford in 1987, combining it with his industrial career. His musical activities since then have included concert promotion, the commissioning of a concert overture, *Orpheus & Bacchus*, by the Welsh composer Daniel Jones (premiered in 1989), and sponsorship of the Guildford Philharmonic Orchestra, for which he won an ABSA award. He brings many perspectives of understanding to help newcomers to classical music; a convert to classical music at the age of 18; a keen record collector for 35 years; the owner and operator of a classical music shop; and the former Strategy Director of Thorn EMI plc, owners of EMI and the HMV retail chain.

Author's Acknowledgements

I am indebted to many people for their contributions to *Discovering Classical Music*. Sharon, my partner and wife, for her support, patience and professional input; George Israel, an artist whose penetrating impressions of the great composers are no doubt influenced by the fact that he has also conducted many of the great operas; Jane Garrett, my editor, for her honest and constructive advice and expertise; and Tim Guy, for his creative and design skills. In addition, Geoffrey and Mary Monk – the ultimate 'good neighbours' – provided timely, valuable, and positive critiques; Nicky Di-Mond was an expert secretary, and Andrew Sanders showed me many ropes.

Sources of information for the first section of each chapter have included: *Johann Sebastian Bach* by Karl Geiringer (George Allen and Unwin); *Mozart in Vienna* by Volkmar Braunberens (Andre Deutsch); *Beethoven* by Dennis Matthews (Dent); *Schubert* by George Marek (Hale); *Berlioz* by Hugh Macdonald (Dent); *Verdi* by Julian Budden (Dent); *Bruckner* by Deryck Cooke (in The New Grove, Macmillan); *Tchaikovsky* by Edward Garden (Dent); *Dvořák* by Neil Butterworth (Omnibus Press); *Mahler* by Michael Kennedy (Dent). I am indebted to these authors and numerous others who have written and researched the lives of these composers. Any errors of interpretation or fact are my responsibility.

Specific acknowledgements for quoted passages are due to:
– *The letters of Mozart and his family* edited by Emily Anderson, published by Macmillan.
– *Selected letters of Gustav Mahler* edited by Knud Martner, published by Faber & Faber.
– *The Human Paradox* by Anthony Mann, published by NMGC.
and the glossary has many debts to the *New Penguin Dictionary of Music* by Arthur Jacobs.

Discovering
CLASSICAL
MUSIC

IAN CHRISTIANS

To Sharon, Sarah, Miranda and Alex

Published by Simply Classics Publications, a division of Simply Classics Limited

Cover and book design by Timothy Guy Design, Truro, Cornwall
Phototypeset on 10/12pt Bembo by Intype, London
Printed by Biddles Limited, Guildford, Surrey

ISBN 0–9518301–0–4

Simply Classics Limited,
Burghley Court, Burghley Road, Wimbledon, London SW19 5BQ

CONTENTS

1

INTRODUCTION

*'Perhaps only music, the most immediate
of all arts, can fully convey the
innermost feelings of sorrow and joy.
There is an innate truth in the language
of music which no words, however
eloquent, can equal'* Anthony Mann

The large part that music, in its many forms, plays in our world today is a recognition of its appeal to our emotions, and this reaches its peak in classical music, with its range and depth of emotional expression and rich variety of instruments.

This book is written to help you enter the magnificent, emotional world of classical music, an entry which is easier than you think, and enormously pleasurable. It is written at a time when classical music is poised to make the big break-through to mass popularity.

It is on this brink in the U.K. today because of three significant events and many subtle trends, which are at last combining to overwhelm the many reactionary forces which have maintained classical music as an exclusive and elitist preserve.

The events that brought classical music to the fore were:

– The film *'Amadeus'*, based on Peter Shaffer's play of the same name, which has done wonders for Mozart's music, making him undoubtedly the most popular of the great composers. *'Amadeus'* was a superb showcase, with a riveting plot, great visual scenes, marvellous music, and a portrayal of Mozart which, if extremely inaccurate, at least made him real.

- Nigel Kennedy's recording of Vivaldi's *Four Seasons*, which got close to becoming Britain's top-selling album in the pop charts, an unprecedented position for Vivaldi and a classical violinist. Kennedy's 'pop image' was important : he consciously changed his presentation from the traditional, conservative soloist, to a somewhat punk and artificially inarticulate Cockney pop star.

- The 1990 World Cup in Italy, and the BBC's choice of an 18-year-old recording of the aria *Nessun Dorma* (None Shall Sleep) from Puccini's opera *Turandot*. This beautiful aria, with its thrilling climax, achieved the ultimate free promotion and audience, and put the larger-than-life Luciano Pavarotti – the world's greatest tenor voice – right at the top of the pop charts. The happy coincidence of 'The Three Greatest Tenors' concert (Pavarotti plus Domingo and Carreras) before the World Cup Final – introducing the prospect of rival fan clubs – has reinforced interest in classical music's closest link with pop stars – the operatic tenor. This success has put Pavarotti truly into the megastar category, a position of great power for enlarging the audience for classical music.

In all three cases, music that has been available for years has been packaged and promoted for the popular market, and has been enormously successful. But as of today, no-one has yet given the '*Amadeus*' treatment to the lives of Beethoven, Berlioz or Schubert; numerous violin concertos with an appeal at least as great as Vivaldi's *Four Seasons* await their turn; dozens of great tenor arias remain stuck in their operas, awaiting much greater recognition. The point is that the popular market has only seen the tip of the iceberg of great music, but it has shown its enthusiasm in a massive way.

The breath of fresh air is welcome, since it undermines all the factors that have kept classical music from its natural audience. Such factors include:

- The unattractive association of classical music with snob value.

- The determined focus of BBC Radio 3 on the traditional serious music lovers, with little interest in programmes for enlarging its audience.

- The past intellectual elitism of some in the classical music industry, who seemed to prefer that it was kept exclusive.

– Classical music has been marketed ineffectively in the past. Anyone entering a shop selling classical music is still presented with a bewildering array of recordings, which range from the appalling to the great in terms of quality of music, performance, and recording, but which usually hide these disparities behind sleeves of pretty pictures which have nothing to do with music at all. What is right for you to buy, as a newcomer to classical music, has historically not been considered, and this is only gradually starting to change.

In the last few years, however, there have also been subtle forces at work to popularise classical music.

– The advertising industry has been familiarizing television viewers with some of the most immediately appealing classical music. Promoting Hovis bread has promoted Dvořák's *New World Symphony*.

– Many successful films ('*Elvira Madigan*', '*Death in Venice*', '*Moonstruck*', to name a few) have used classical music as an integral part.

– Extraordinary developments in technology have resulted in high fidelity sound reproduction (so-called Hi-Fi) being available at a fraction of the cost of a few years ago. The sound of a glorious orchestra – so vivid, varied and dynamically extreme – can now be realistically recreated in your home at widely affordable prices.

– The magical compact disc, which has at last taken physical contact out of sound reproduction, with its silent background, wider dynamic range, doubled playing time, and relative indestructability, is a sound-carrier designed, above all, for classical music. For example, you no longer need to get up and change sides three times, but can sit right through the 80 minutes of Gustav Mahler's powerful *Resurrection Symphony*. It is the next best thing to the concert hall.

– The pricing strategies of the main classical music companies, Polygram (which owns Phillips, D.G.G. and Decca) and EMI are positively generous. After the initial launch of classical C.D.s at £9.99 in 1983, the top price has gone up by forty per cent (whilst inflation has increased by sixty per cent), and mid-price and budget price C.D.s have been introduced at £9 and £6 or less. With the previously mentioned C.D. benefits, classical music has never sounded better nor been more affordable, particularly when you appreciate the bizarre fact that quality and price are not related! By this I mean that the best is often cheaper than the rest! To give an example, again using Mahler's *Resurrection Symphony*, the historically acclaimed recording by the great conductor, and Mahler protégé, Otto Klemperer, is available for £9, whilst the alternatives range from £13 to £25. There are hundreds of other examples, where you can get fabulous bargains.

So, the time is now absolutely ripe for introducing classical music in a much wider audience, at bargain prices, and this book is written to help it happen for you. If you are uncertain how to approach classical music, where to start, where to proceed, what to buy, and, importantly, how to enjoy it, you should find this book helpful.

On the path of discovery in classical music, you have taken the first critical step – you have bought the book, and it is likely that music is, in some way, important in your life. In addition, all that is required is that you are honest with yourself about what you like and don't like; that you are prepared to take risks and try the unknown; and that you allow yourself time to get to know your discoveries, since familiarity vastly adds to enjoyment.

This book is based on three fundamental beliefs, that:

– What you like is the key to your discovery path into classical music.

– There is an almost endless selection of music that you will like, provided you take it one step at a time.

– Knowing about the personalities and lives of the great composers enhances enjoyment and provides an attractive road of discovery.

This book is written to lead you, whatever your preferences, to the most enjoyable music for you. It will provide a good, though far from total, grounding in the music of ten great composers. But once you get to the point of going further, let good biographies and your own judgment be your guide.

2

CLASSICAL COMPOSERS
ARE THE STARS

*T*wo of the main factors in popularising classical music involved treating the artists, Kennedy and Pavarotti, as pop stars. Regrettably, collecting their recordings is a very limiting method of exploring classical music, since their specialisations cover only a fraction of the repertoire.

In the film '*Amadeus*', however, Mozart was the star, and as a result the awareness of Mozart dramatically increased. So did the sales of all his music! Many people discovered the music for the first time, and when they went to buy it, the identity of the performers was the least important factor. The 'classical composers are the stars' philosophy is inherently much more appropriate to discovering classical music than the limiting 'the artist is the star' approach which derives from pop music. It is more appropriate too than cherry-picking any individual works which have appeal but where the identity of the composer is essentially irrelevant.

In following the 'composers are the stars' approach you gain familiarity with the composer, you come to know his musical style and are led towards a broad variety of works. The composer ceases to be a name from the past, but becomes a human being with a gift for powerful communication. In consequence the music lives much more.

The fascination of Mozart's life is not unique. Beethoven, Berlioz, Wagner each had amazing lives; Bach and Haydn were great men; Schumann's extreme sensitivity drove him mad; Tchaikovsky – a homosexual – committed suicide in the most bizarre circumstances, and so on. Finding out the details of the lives of these great composers, who still give so much pleasure today, not only helps enormously as you listen to their music, but is also extremely interesting in itself. In some cases 'to know is to love', and listening to the music of Mozart, Beethoven, Berlioz and Bruckner becomes particularly special when you are aware of the adversities they faced and the sort of people they were.

The number of composers who have made their mark on a significant scale over the years might run into three figures, but it is still a relatively small number. Amongst them are a small number of absolute geniuses, who are household names today. In this book I have chosen ten great composers, a number that is sufficient for variety, and not excessive for your attention. I have chosen them to give a coverage of the period from the beginning of the 18th century to the beginning of the 20th; to ensure no form of music (e.g. opera) is ignored; and above all to ensure that newcomers to classical music find that there is a wealth of easily accessible music.

There is no truly modern music in this book, I prefer you to come to that via Mahler, who is sufficiently modern for this first volume. Many famous composers (e.g. Haydn, Brahms) are deferred to the next book in the interests of variety in this one. On the following pages in this chapter, you will see listings of the greatest composers of the last three centuries, so that you can become, if necessary, familiar with their names and period.

Each chapter on a composer follows the following structure

– an ink-drawing portrait of the composer

– a short history of the composer's life

– a view of the composer as a person

– a step-by-step guide into the composer's music

Of the ten composers, Mozart and Beethoven stand out for the breadth of their works, as well as their ability to achieve an immediate and positive response to their music. They were both extremely versatile, and their music provides a marvellous opportunity to explore the relative attractions of symphonies, concertos, operas, choral works, chamber music and solo instruments.

For this reason the chapters on Mozart and Beethoven come first, and then the order reverts to a chronological sequence for the remaining eight composers. The book is completed by two chapters, one that describes the importance of artists and interpretation to your enjoyment, and the other on how to eliminate the confusion in buying recordings of classical music.

GREAT COMPOSERS OF
THE EIGHTEENTH CENTURY

1700   1750   1800

Vivaldi
1675–1741

Highly prolific and innovative Italian baroque composer. Popularity of "The Four Seasons" has unjustly swamped the rest of his work.

J. S. Bach
1685–1750

See Chapter 5.

Handel
1685–1759

German born genius who lived in England for the second half of his life. Very prolific in operas and oratorios.

Haydn
1732–1809

Very productive Austrian composer of genius, and a great person too. Wrote over a hundred symphonies of exceptional overall quality.

Mozart
1756–1791

See Chapter 3.

GREAT COMPOSERS OF
THE NINETEENTH CENTURY

1800   1850   1900

Beethoven 1770–1827	See Chapter 4.
Rossini 1792–1868	Brilliant Italian opera composer who retired rich in his thirties.
Schubert 1797–1828	See Chapter 6.
Berlioz 1803–1869	See Chapter 7.
Mendelssohn 1809–1847	A German child prodigy who wrote some of his best works in his teens.
Schumann 1810–1856	Highly gifted German romantic composer who died insane.
Chopin 1810–1849	Great Polish pianist and composer for the instrument, with a unique style.
Liszt 1811–1886	A great piano virtuoso, who composed some magnificent works for his instrument.
Wagner 1813–1883	Egocentric German genius who composed great but long operas.
Verdi 1813–1901	See Chapter 8.
Bruckner 1824–1896	See Chapter 9.
Brahms 1833–1897	A great and serious German composer with high standards and inhibitions.
Tchaikovsky 1840–1893	See Chapter 10.
Dvořák 1841–1904	See Chapter 11.

GREAT COMPOSERS OF
THE TWENTIETH CENTURY

1900   1950   1990

Janáček 1854-1925	A Czech composer of startling originality, whose talents developed right up until his death.
Elgar 1857-1934	English self-taught composer, who wrote powerful and emotional music.
Puccini 1858-1924	An Italian operatic master whose popular works are full of emotion, action and great melodies.
Mahler 1860-1911	See Chapter 12.
Debussy 1862-1918	French 'impressionist' composer and innovator.
Richard Strauss 1864-1949	A German composer, mainly of tone poems and opera, whose heart was in the nineteenth century.
Nielsen 1865-1931	A Danish composer of originality, particularly in his symphonies.
Sibelius 1865-1957	A Finnish nationalist composer of highly individualistic but accessible music.
Vaughan Williams 1872-1958	A very English composer who used folk themes extensively.
Rachmaninov 1873-1943	A passionate Russian in the Tchaikovsky mould, who wrote some magnificent symphonies and piano works.
Schoenberg 1874-1951	Revolutionary composer who created the "twelve-note" method of modern music.
Ravel 1875-1937	Overlapped with Debussy, and also a French "impressionist" composer.
Bartók 1881-1941	Hungarian nationalist composer who used folk music extensively . Modern and rhythmic.
Stravinsky 1882-1971	Highly original Russian composer whose "modern" music has become a natural part of the repertoire.
Prokofiev 1891-1953	A Russian composer of modern, original style, with some works having wide appeal.
Shostakovich 1906-1975	A great Russian composer, who is Mahler's heir as a symphonist.
Britten 1913-1976	An English composer, with an extensive output, covering many different types of work.

3

MOZART

Mozart *His Life*

*W*olfgang Amadeus Mozart was born on January 29, 1756, in Salzburg, Austria. His father, Leopold, was a musician at the court of the Prince and Archbishop of Salzburg. His mother, Maria Anna, had seven children, but only Wolfgang, the last boy, and his sister Nannerl, five years older, survived infancy.

Leopold Mozart was an extremely ambitious and very competent musician. He was highly intelligent, very well read, and kept himself well informed of a wide range of events in Europe. Teaching was perhaps his forte (he wrote a famous treatise on playing the violin) and his great desire to develop a child prodigy was rewarded by having an enormously gifted son. From the beginning, music was the young Mozart's greatest delight.

Having a child prodigy for a son meant that Leopold was able to break away from an extremely limited life, effectively as a servant at the court. Leopold was an excellent business and tour manager, and after six years of teaching Mozart the clavier – the ancestor of the modern piano – and the violin, the travels started – first Munich, then Vienna, where they were summoned to the Emperor's palace and Mozart's fame and reputation were launched. The commercial rewards for entertaining the nobility were gifts such as jewellery, and only occasionally money.

In 1763, the family set off on a tour of Europe that was to last three and a half years and encompass Paris and London. The young Mozart was welcomed and applauded by kings, queens, princes and princesses, and it was during this period that his first compositions were published. During the 15 months in London, Mozart enriched his musical experience by meeting Johann Christian Bach – the great Johann Sebastian Bach's youngest son and a composer of wide taste. Mozart's first symphony was written at this time. By 1767, Wolfgang Amadeus Mozart was famous throughout Europe as the greatest performing musical prodigy ever seen, and furthermore 'handsome, vivacious, graceful and full of good manners'.

Mozart now turned to opera, which he preferred, even at this time, to all other forms of music. At the end of 1769 he and his father were off to Italy, where he was created a Knight of the Golden Spur, a high honour, and was also elected to the prestigious Accademia Filarmonica at Bologna, the youngest member ever. Mozart had a commission to write an opera, *Mitradate*, for Milan. This provided him with a great success, and he returned to Salzburg in 1771 a famous composer.

The rest of the 1770s were years of lower profile for Mozart. Now in his teens, he no longer stood out so obviously as a prodigy. Leopold was disappointed that he was unable to obtain for his gifted son the important position in a European court which would provide the security he felt so important. But Mozart was enjoying successes with his early operas *Lucio Silla* and *La Finta Giardiniera*, commissioned for Milan and Munich.

Above all, his compositions in all forms – serenades, concertos, symphonies, choral works, chamber music and operas – provided the essential experience and development necessary to produce the great masterpieces of the 1780s and the last two years of his life.

Nonetheless, by any standards, the Mozart compositions of the seventies include many outstanding works, including the exquisite *Symphony No.29* and the *Haffner Serenade*. But life at Salzburg was increasingly trying. The old Archbishop had died in 1771 and been succeeded by Prince Colloredo – neither a great music-lover nor a lover of musicians – who had no interest in helping Mozart's ambitions.

In 1777, Leopold petitioned Colloredo to be allowed to undertake another tour with his son. The Archbishop at first turned them down and then sacked them. This threw Leopold into such a state that he was forced to beg for his job back.

In the end, Mozart went off on an ill-fated tour with his mother. This tour was Mozart's coming of age, as, for the first time, he had to manage without his father. Yet again, it failed to provide him with a suitable position or money (useless gifts were still the typical reward for performing for the nobility) and led him and his elderly mother from one disappointment to another – ultimately to his mother's death in Paris.

The high spot of the tour for Mozart was his meeting with the Weber family in Mannheim. The Webers were a poor, but artistic, family. The father (who died in 1779) preferred to be a musician than a bureaucrat, and three of the four daughters became singers. Mozart fell in love with Aloysia, the second of the four daughters, who had an outstanding voice. In spite of being rejected by her, he became part of the family, and five years later married Aloysia's sister, Constanze.

From Paris it was back to Salzburg and, amazingly, to an Archbishop keen to employ him – still an unattractive proposition for Mozart, but a stable existence after his disappointing travels. During this period he composed steadily, with masterpieces including the *Sinfonia Concertante for violin and viola*.

The catalyst for the breakout from Salzburg was a commission from the Elector of Munich to write an opera, *Idomeneo, King of Crete*. Mozart travelled to Munich for this in November 1780, and the opera, first performed the following January, was his greatest triumph to date.

Fate had Mozart move on to Vienna, summoned by the Archbishop, and it was with the confidence of *Idomeneo* behind him that he travelled to the high capital of music, which was to be his home for the rest of his life. In great demand by the Austrian nobility, who remembered his visits as a child prodigy, Mozart was also accepted into the highest circles of Viennese society, meeting them on an equal basis. It was a stark contrast with life at the Colloredo residence, where he was treated like a menial servant, eating with the valets and cooks.

Mozart's final confrontation with Colloredo came just before the Archbishop's retinue was due to return to Salzburg. After a great row, Mozart resigned – although Archbishop Colloredo never officially accepted his resignation. Antipathy to Colloredo (a feeling that was mutual), self-respect, the prospect of being a star in Vienna, and the fact that the Weber family was now living there, were the main factors in this rupture. The final departure, a few weeks later, conjures up a lovely picture – the Archbishop's Chamberlain, Count Arco (who was actually a friend of the Mozart family), finally losing his temper, calling Mozart a clown and knave, and tossing him out of the room, in Mozart's words: 'with a kick in the ass'.

For Mozart, it was a break with the tradition of composers working for the aristocracy, leaving him in the vulnerable position of freelance composer, music director and pianoforte soloist in a cultural capital renowned for its high political intrigues.

At first, Mozart rented lodgings from the Weber family. He planned to make money from giving concerts and taking on pupils, whilst seeking a commission to write an opera. This happened almost immediately: *Die Entführung aus dem Serail*, (The Abduction from the Harem) was commenced in August 1781.

On December 24, Mozart was invited by the Emperor Joseph II to play in a competition against the famous Italian composer Clementi. Clementi, who mistook Mozart for an Imperial Chamberlain when he first met him, came a resounding second, much to the Emperor's delight. This shows how well established Mozart had become.

Mozart now fell in love with Constanze, the third of the Weber daughters, aged 19. He described her as 'not ugly, but at the same time far from beautiful. Her whole beauty consists in two little black eyes and a pretty figure', in a letter to his father, who still tried to keep his son on the straight and narrow, and did not approve of the Bohemian Webers. Because Mozart was hard up, he and Constanze were unable to get married until August 1782, after the success of *Die Entführung*, which was first performed on July 16.

Mozart's life now became more settled. He was well established in Viennese society, and earned a lot more than he had while working for Archbishop Colloredo. He composed regularly for his subscription concerts and for commissions that he received. He also played in the salons of some of his friends in the aristocracy, such as the Countess Thun – everyone who was anyone, including the Emperor, came to her 'open house' evening.

Mozart moved home frequently, according to the space he needed – for pianos, for teaching and for his impending family – and his financial circumstances. He lived an extraordinarily full life. 'Last week I gave a ball in my rooms . . . we began at six o'clock and kept on until seven. What! Only an hour? Of course not. I meant until seven o'clock next morning' he wrote in a letter to his father. All the time he was composing music, which was now regularly attaining inspired levels, as well as giving concerts.

14

His first child was born in June 1783, but died shortly after. Altogether Constanze was to give birth to six children, of whom only two, Karl (born in 1784) and Franz (born in 1791) were to survive infancy. In September, Mozart and Constanze made their only visit to Salzburg, where she sang in the first performance of Mozart's great, but unfinished, *C Minor Mass*. On their return trip to Vienna, they stopped off at Linz and in just four days Mozart composed his *Symphony No.36* which has taken the name of its birthplace.

1784 was the year in which Mozart's friendship with Haydn developed. Haydn, another musical genius, was a generous and honest man, who became a father figure to him. They undoubtedly learned from, and inspired, each other, in a unique relationship. When Mozart's father visited Salzburg the following year, Haydn told him 'Before God, your son is the greatest composer known to me.' One of the first flowerings of the relationship was an outstanding set of six string quartets which Mozart dedicated to Haydn.

Leopold's ten week visit to Vienna in 1785 was a great success, packed with activity. It was here that he was able, at last, to appreciate his son's success, and these extracts from letters to his daughter back in Salzburg capture events marvellously:

> *The concert was magnificent . . . we had a new and very fine concerto by Wolfgang, which the copyist was still copying when we arrived.*

> *Your brother played a glorious concerto . . . I was sitting only two boxes from the beautiful Princess of Wurttemberg and had the great pleasure of hearing so clearly all the interplay of instruments that for sheer delight tears came into my eyes. When your brother left the platform the Emperor waved his hat and called out 'Bravo, Mozart!'*

> *We never get to bed before one o'clock . . . Every day there are concerts; and the whole time is given up to teaching, music, composing and so forth . . . It is impossible for me to describe the hustle and bustle . . . Your brother's forte piano has been taken at least a dozen times to the theatre or to some other house.*

At last, in 1785, Mozart was able to find a play and librettist able to provide a challenging opera libretto. *The Marriage of Figaro* was highly topical and controversial, being 'anti' the aristocracy (the French Revolution was just round the corner). Lorenzo da Ponte, who created the libretto, was an Italian poet who had led a life nearly as fascinating as the great lover, Casanova. In due course he was also to provide Mozart with the librettos for two more great operas, *Don Giovanni* and *Cosi fan Tutte*. *The Marriage of Figaro* was first performed on May 1, 1786. Political feelings ran high, and not a few people hoped for its failure. In the event the opera was only a moderate success, being a completely new concept, contemporary and controversial, and the aristocracy did not like its republican tendencies.

It was only when *The Marriage of Figaro* was produced in Prague, later that year, that it achieved great success. In fact, the citizens of Prague appreciated Mozart and his music much more than the Viennese. As Mozart described it 'Here they talk about nothing but *Figaro*. Nothing is played, sung or whistled but *Figaro*. No opera is drawing like *Figaro*. Nothing, nothing but *Figaro*. Certainly a great honour for me!' Another opera, *Don Giovanni*, was immediately commissioned by Prague.

On May 28, 1787, whilst Mozart was at work on *Don Giovanni*, his father Leopold died. At the end of that year Mozart was back in Prague for its first performance – a 'triumphant success'. Shortly afterwards he was appointed 'Chamber Composer' to encourage him to remain in Vienna – his first and only court appointment.

Mozart's three last great symphonies (*Nos. 39–41*) were written the next year, and it was at this time that his need to borrow money first appeared. He also lost his six-month-old daughter. Much is made of Mozart's straitened circumstances in his last years. Undoubtedly he was severely strapped for cash at certain times, but he still earned a considerable amount of money, in spite of the severe curtailment of funds available for music in Vienna: the Turkish war, which started in the summer of 1787, had become a severe drain on the economy. Fewer concerts, fewer operas, fewer commissions were given, and private orchestras were disbanded. Constanze became ill, and needed expensive cures at the spa of Baden. There was also a mysterious problem, referred to in his letters only as 'the matter you know of', which could indicate a totally unknown financial difficulty.

Mozart made one of his longer trips abroad, to Berlin, in April 1789, travelling with his friend, Prince Lichnowsky. The trip does not seem to have been a great success, though Mozart probably played before the King of Prussia, and he received commissions for six string quartets and six piano sonatas (a commission he never completed). On his return, Constanze became very seriously ill, but although these were far less happy times than a few years earlier, Mozart's output of great music continued unabated. His final opera written in collaboration with Lorenzo da Ponte, *Cosi fan Tutte*, (All women are the same), was written at this time for the Court, but sadly the Emperor died without seeing it.

The new Emperor, Leopold, was not a music lover, and Mozart's petition to become second Kapellmeister (music director) to Salieri failed. Salieri was the most powerful composer in Vienna at this time. With this change of climate, Mozart needed to take a new direction, particularly as his friends at court were being replaced by Leopold's choices. A visit to England was an attractive option – regrettably not realised – but he undertook a commission to write a popular German opera, *The Magic Flute*, for his friend, the talented impresario Emanuel Schikaneder. This opera was a great commercial success and played to a far wider audience than Mozart's other Viennese opera productions. Mozart took Salieri and Salieri's mistress, the singer Madame Cavalieri, to see it – Salieri loved it! This wasn't Mozart's last opera, he undertook to write one to celebrate the coronation of Leopold as King of Bohemia in Prague. This was a return to old fashioned opera, based on Roman themes, and Mozart rattled off the music of *La Clemenza da Tito* (The Clemency of Titus) within two months, interrupting work on the anonymous commission of a Requiem Mass.

Mozart's health was always a little fragile, although he managed to live an extremely hectic life, but around November 20, 1791, he fell seriously ill. His hands and feet started to swell and he was soon unable to move. His sister-in-law described the last night (December 4/5) vividly: 'Süssmayr was at Mozart's bedside. The well-known *Requiem* lay on the quilt and Mozart was explaining to him how, in his opinion, he ought to finish it when he was gone. He also urged his wife to keep his death a secret until she informed Albrechtsberger, who was in charge of all the services at the cathedral. A long search was made for Dr. Closset, who was found at the opera but who had to wait for the end of the performance. He came and ordered cold compresses to be placed on Mozart's burning head, which, however, affected him to such an extent that he became unconscious and remained so until he died. His last movement was an attempt to express with his mouth the drum passage in the *Requiem*. That I can still hear'.

Mozart died at one o'clock in the morning with death caused by rheumatic fever. His funeral, a private one, was held in St. Stephen's Church on December 7. In keeping with contemporary practice, he was given a third-class burial in a shared grave whose location is unknown (and which would have been re-used within ten years anyway).

Many dramatic stories have been created around the tragic, early death of Mozart and his burial. Poisoning and a pauper's grave make a dramatic story, but the latest research refutes both.

Mozart's death was reported thus in the Vienna press, 'His works, which are loved and admired everywhere, are proof of his greatness – and they reveal the irreplaceable loss which the noble art of music has suffered through his death.' Haydn said 'We shall not see such a talent again in a 100 years'.

As might be expected, Prague paid the greatest homage to Mozart, on December 14. A newspaper described the event: 'On that day all the bells of the church were rung for half an hour; almost the entire city turned out, so that the square in front of the church could not accommodate all the coaches, and neither could the church accommodate all the admirers of the departed composer, although it has room for almost 4,000 people. The Requiem was by the Kapellmeister Rössler, and was superbly performed by 120 leading musicians, at the head of whom was the beloved singer Madame Duschek. In the middle of the church stood a magnificently illuminated catafalque; three choirs of trumpets and drums sounded mournful strains; the Requiem mass was celebrated by Father Rudolf Fischer; 12 students from the local grammar school carried torches, with black crepe over their shoulders and white cloths in their hands. A solemn stillness prevailed, and countless tears flowed in painful remembrance of that artist whose harmonies had so often moved our hearts to joy.'

Mozart *The Person*

Mozart was 'A remarkably small man, with a profusion of fine, fair hair' according to his friend Michael Kelly. He liked to dress well, and was a little vain about his appearance. He was highly intelligent, and a very spontaneous person. Fun-loving, he always retained a young person's sense of humour, and an ability to let his hair down. He loved to drink punch, for which he had a considerable capacity, and to play billiards, a game at which he was an expert.

Mozart retained, along with his high degree of sophistication, an adolescent's delight in the vulgar or basic, as his letters show. Prim he was not!

He was not concerned too much by other people's reactions, and they could think him immature and irresponsible. He could get ideas that were unrealistic, and he was not very commercially minded. He was poor at the politics so necessary for success at Court. He could be prickly. Nevertheless, few people were in doubt that he was a genius, and he was well aware of his gifts.

In musical matters he always had supreme self-confidence. His professional judgement of people was devastatingly blunt – and accurate. The contrast between his early life of being hailed by royalty abroad, and later treated as a servant in Salzburg, gave him quite a resentment of the aristocracy, a resentment that was never far below the surface. Hence he particularly delighted in his enormous popularity with the citizens of Prague.

He had a strong set of ethical values. He was a loving and faithful husband. He was an outstanding professional, extremely hard-working, with a fabulous ear. He had great intuitive insights into human nature, as shown in his operas, but he didn't always recognise them or apply them in his own life. His father was always a powerful and critical influence, and whilst Mozart did seek his father's approval, he definitely wanted to lead his own life. Leopold's influence did, however, hold the wilder side of Mozart in restraint.

Mozart was, above all, an artist, and music dominated his whole life. His family, billiards, parties, his travels, and the problems – mainly financial – that he created for himself, filled in the gaps. But even on his death-bed he was still composing!

Mozart *His Music*

Mozart was an exceptionally gifted composer, and before his death at the early age of 35 he had composed an amazing number of master-pieces. He was the right person in the right environment – born with the potential for genius, the only son of an extremely talented musician, composer and teacher, who also had the vision and ambition to create a musical genius applauded throughout Europe.

Whilst many great composers took years to reach their full flowering, Mozart began creating masterpieces in his teens. He had a great head-start, composing from the age of six, and in the hot-house environment created by his father, he had written full operas at the age of 12. With his intelligence, musical gifts and experience, everything was accelerated, and combined with his high motivation to compose, he produced more in his short life than others might do in a full 70 years.

Mozart's great love was opera, and he developed an extraordinary talent for composing for the voice and orchestra. With his highly sensi-tive ear, he would write the final form of an aria only when he heard the voice of his singer. His own performing talent was the piano (he was a good violinist too). He was the greatest player of his time, and he wrote his magnificent series of piano concertos for his own performance.

Don't be fooled by the stately elegance of Mozart's music into think-ing of it as 'pretty music'. It is beautiful, but it is also dramatic. Listen to the way in which he uses the orchestra, and particularly the wood-wind, to produce the most remarkable communication of joy, sadness, and poignancy. The oboe, flute, clarinet, bassoon and horn become like human voices, singing songs without words, nowhere more than in the orchestral accompaniment in the piano concertos.

Mozart's output was prodigious, 626 works are identified in the official catalogue prepared by Köchel. Each of his compositions is ident-ified by a K-number, for example his last work, the *Requiem*, is K626. Mozart's output over time is shown in the following chart.

Age and output

Mozart's age	10	20	25	30	35
Köchel number	*30*	*250*	*375*	*500*	*626*

He wrote in every form – many concertos and symphonies for the concert hall; operas for the theatre; settings of religious music for church services; serenades, sonatas, and different forms of chamber music principally for salons.

So, first the 'Mozart Starterpack' to introduce you to the composer! To do justice to Mozart and yourself, I recommend that you start on a broad front to enable you to decide where you wish to explore further. I suggest that you approach five works representing five different aspects of Mozart's music:

1 Piano Concertos My first recommendation is to listen to *Piano Concerto No.22* (K 482). It has one of Mozart's most dramatic first movements. Almost immediately the woodwind instruments start tossing the opening theme between themselves, before the rest of the orchestra asserts itself in a strongly rhythmic and attractive second theme to which the music keeps returning. The slow movement is beautiful and serious, with a glorious mini-serenade for the woodwind in the middle. The concluding movement is exquisite, in turns swinging and delicate. This is the sort of music that, as Leopold described it in Vienna, brings tears to your eyes with its sheer beauty.

2 Symphonies The *Jupiter Symphony*, so-called for its Olympian qualities, is Mozart's last. From its opening arresting bars it projects great elegance and power. The rhythms are insistent, driving the opening movement on after the introduction of a sweetly contrasting theme. Trumpets and drums add a marvellous ceremonial touch. A beautiful, flowing slow movement, conveying a mood of great tranquillity, is followed by an outstandingly languid minuet which forces you to sway to its elegantly simple waltz-like rhythm. The finale is Mozart's symphonic 'tour-de-force'. Brilliant and exciting, his themes are interwoven in the orchestra at a marvellous pace, and the symphony comes to a conclusion that should bring the house down – or the audience to its feet. After a magnificent fugue, in which each string section takes up the same theme at intervals, the orchestra breaks free and rushes into the home straight to cross the finishing line with a joyful fanfare of trumpets.

3 Opera You don't need to start with a whole opera, as you can acquire excerpts, the best bits. *The Magic Flute*, a sensational success in its time, operates on two levels – the exalted and noble, and the human and comical. It combines two love stories, Tamino and Pamina (the hero and heroine), and Papageno and Papagena (the bird-catcher and his longed-for mate). The music therefore provides strong contrasts, but Mozart's magical tunes are shared equally between the serious lovers and their comic counterparts. Papageno's songs *The bird-catcher am I*, and *A sweetheart or a wife is what Papageno wants* are delightful and world famous. (The English translations nearly always sound unnecessarily off-putting!) The scene where he considers suicide, is dissuaded at the last moment, and plays his magic bells to attract a soul-mate (Papagena) is hilarious, as is their joyous duet – which starts with tentative getting-to-know-you 'Pa-Pa's. One senses that Mozart identified more with Papageno than Tamino. Other highlights include the Queen of the Night's phenomenal coloratura (ornate) singing (first performed by Mozart's sister-in-law), a glass-shattering feat of vocal gymnastics, and the hymn *O Isis and Osiris* is just one of several noble choral numbers. The *Magic Flute* is a fabulous, richly melodic opera, with a strong touch of pantomime, but as with all Mozart's great operas it is what you want it to be. It is best heard without the German speaking parts between the music.

4 Chamber Music For a more intimate view of Mozart's music, the *String Quintet in C*, K515, is hauntingly beautiful. This is late night music, when the hurly-burly of the day is over. The first movement starts with great authority and a totally clear part for each instrument. Two violins, viola and cello – the standard string quartet – are augmented by a second viola. The magical and extraordinarily simple themes build to a climax out of which comes the most exquisite musing theme in a dying fall, which ultimately ends the movement. This is my favourite first movement of all chamber music. The following adagio is passionate, beautiful, and very moving. After a minuet which starts languidly, but quickly gets geared up, the quintet ends with a dashing and witty finale. This is chamber music at its very best.

5 Choral Music Mozart's last and unfinished work, the *Requiem*, is a powerful and dark piece, all the more moving for the circumstances whereby it became his own Requiem, unfinished on his death-bed and commissioned by a mysterious, anonymous patron. All Mozart's mastery is brought to bear on this, his first substantial sacred work for many years, and with the choral singing creating its own special fervour, the impact is formidable. It opens with sombre orchestration and mood. Throughout, Mozart exercises a controlled severity with the religious text. The intensity builds to a high pitch in the *Dies Irae* (Day of wrath) with its fast-running and powerful rhythms. The solo trombone at *Tuba Mirum* (the trumpets shall sound) is a master stroke as is the *Confutatis Maledictus* (the damned shall be confounded), with its fiery and persistent representation of the damned, set against a beautiful prayer for salvation. Afterwards there is the sublime *Lacrimosa* (mournful), where Mozart finally laid down his pen. Its poignancy is much magnified as a result. Only musicologists could tell that Mozart's assistant, Süssmayer, completed the work.

These very different examples of his works will give you a sense of the great breadth of Mozart's output, and the unique style and character of his musical 'fingerprint'. It will also allow you to gauge your response to it, particularly when you become familiar with each work. I hope this initial contact with Mozart's genius will lead you on a marvellous voyage of discovery through his great compositions. The landmarks of that voyage are laid out for you now. Follow the route based on your own preferences, which will of course develop as you progress, and do read to the end of this chapter before making your first choices.

Piano concertos

Mozart's piano concertos from *No.9* to *No.27* are eventually going to end up in any Mozart lover's collection, since they are all masterpieces and if you like one, you are almost certain to like the rest. However, there are five that are amongst the greatest and the most easily accessible:

No. 17 K453 The first movement opens very elegantly, but quickly plunges into a dramatic orchestral statement, with woodwind prominent. Throughout the movement, the drama and gentle beauty provide exciting contrast. The slow movement is a most moving and tender andante. A gentle and very brief opening phrase on the strings is followed, after a pause, by a heart-breaking entry of the oboe, in turn followed by the rest of the woodwind – and that's just the start: its magical. The concerto concludes with a cheerful allegretto (moderately fast movement), with delightful interplay between all the instruments. Just before they get carried away with their own musings, Mozart calls a halt, and stirring horn calls lead the concerto to an exhilarating conclusion.

No. 21 K467 Featured in the film '*Elvira Madigan*', it is particularly well known, and justly so. The quiet opening quickly builds into a majestic and martial climax. The piano plays a relatively low profile role in comparison to this orchestral part, but has a memorable and lyrical second theme. The show-stopper, however, is the slow movement, which is gloriously rapt and extremely romantic. This is one of the greatest Mozart movements. The last movement sustains the total quality of the concerto, nearly as powerful as the opening at times, but with delicious humour abounding.

No. 20 K466 This concerto is different! Written in the dramatic key of D minor, its brooding introduction heralds a first movement of great drama and power, unprecedented at the time – a precursor of Beethoven's style. The movement dies away eerily. The slow movement starts in a very different mood with one of Mozart's unforgettable simple themes. The tranquillity is interrupted by an agitated minor key passage before the piano and orchestra return to the opening theme, and then the piano quickly leads into an energetic last movement, still in the minor key and maintaining a serious mood until close to the end, when the music switches totally with a change to the major key and a joyous ending.

No. 23 K488 One of Mozart's happiest concertos, it positively bursts with memorable tunes and makes you feel good to be alive. The first movement relies on melody rather than drama, and is full of lovely touches. The slow movement is in a wistful minor key, but has a singing interlude in the major. The last movement is exuberant, with woodwind flirting with the piano, and then the piano leads the orchestra to a joyful climax.

No. 27 K595 Mozart's last piano concerto opens with breath-taking simplicity, even for him. The first movement has extraordinary grace, and a degree of introspection new to the series. A hushed slow movement maintains the quality and the mood. The last movement opens with a lovely, languid theme, and although it develops dramatically, it is in this same languid mood that this jewel of a work ultimately ends.

24

The remaining Vienna concertos, *Nos.18,19,24,25,26*, are no less fine, and I commend them to you unreservedly, at your leisure. For me, in all the concerto repertoire there is no finer set of works than these. The earlier concertos in the series are not far behind in quality, and the *Double Concerto* (K365) is an exciting, and different, addition. The sound of the two pianos in such a melodic work is unique.

Symphonies

Although Mozart wrote over forty symphonies, the majority are works of his youth. *Symphony No.25* is the first substantial one: it is dramatic, as befits its G minor key, and was heavily featured in the film '*Amadeus*'.

The gem from the early works, *Symphony No.29*, was written a little later, and its true stature is best heard when the opening movement is not rushed. A gentle opening leads to marvellous interplay between the different string sections, and the sound of the elegant theme is fabulously rich. The bold but controlled first movement is followed by a serene and stately andante, then a formal minuet. Finally an exuberant 'allegro con spirito' finale introduces a theme with a terrific swing, and at the end the horns challenge the strings in an exhilarating climax. For me it seems to capture current day fantasies of the late 18th century in Vienna.

The symphonies between *Nos.29* and *35* may not have quite the same appeal, – the finest are *Nos.31, 33*, and *34* – but the last six, from *Nos.35* to *41* (*No.37* was discovered to be by Michael Haydn) are on an ascending scale of true greatness.

No. 35 K385 known as the *Haffner*, is a particularly happy work, and a good bridge from *No.29* to the powerful later symphonies. After an arresting opening, it rushes merrily along, with a great swing and humour. A lovely slow movement, where you can picture 18th century be-wigged couples in a flirtatious dance, is followed by a stately minuet with a glorious middle section. A fast and exuberant finale brings the work to an exciting conclusion.

No. 36 K425 is known as the *Linz* because Mozart completed it in a few days for performance in that city. A noble slow introduction leads to a lively allegro with strong rhythms and delicate contrasts. The slow movement is like a beautiful Mozart opera aria without the singer, high praise, and the symphony continues through the minuet to the lively finale, which bustles and whirls to round off a thoroughly enjoyable work.

No. 38 K504 is nicknamed the *Prague* after the city where it had its first performance. This is a mighty composition, with a powerful introduction setting the scene for a dramatic first movement on a scale beyond any previous Mozart symphony. The strings enjoy fierce interplay before melting into a beautiful second theme in this exciting opening. It is followed by an andante which combines both grace and power. The finale (no minuet in this symphony) starts quietly and quickly, with a catchy melody, but soon gathers momentum. It is full of fun, a foil to the preceding movements.

No. 39 K543 This, the first of the three great and contrasting symphonies written in the summer of 1788, is of a similar style to the *Prague*. It too has a noble adagio introduction, and it dies away into a gentle theme which launches the main allegro. It alternates drama and gentleness to striking effect. The slow movement starts with a hushed, rapt melody, which moves on, after an orchestral hiatus, to an even lovelier theme. This time Mozart had time to write a minuet, a marvellous one with a captivating middle section for his favourite wind instruments. It is followed by a joyful, playful finale, with the woodwind behaving like unruly children.

No. 40 K550 The *G minor Symphony* with its famous opening is of very different mood – serious. A quiet, brooding opening – there is no introduction – sets the scene for this passionate work, with its pervasive rhythms. A sombre slow movement of deceptive simplicity and elegance is followed by a dramatic minuet, broken briefly by a tranquil middle section – the only mood break in the symphony. The memorable last movement maintains strong rhythms and its minor key to the end, at which time you can feel quite unsettled by this remarkable work.

There are many delightful experiences in the early symphonies, for example the last movement of the little known No.28 is pure magic, with one of those enthralling, innocent themes that are the hallmark of Mozart's genius.

Opera

After the fun and solemnity of the *Magic Flute*, Mozart has very different delights in store in his other famous operas!

First, *Don Giovanni*, the dramatic saga of the dissolute rake, which reaches an enthralling climax when the anti-hero is dragged down to hell by the statue of his lover's father, whom he has murdered. Between the overture and the dramatic ending there is a fund of wonderful music – the fizzing *Champagne Aria*, the seductive and beautiful love song *La ci darem la mano* (There you will give me your hand), the exquisite *Il mio tesoro* (My treasure) – and the superb ensembles where all the main characters are singing. In a great performance, the excitement of the last scene, when the statue appears for dinner and bears down on Don Giovanni, can put you on the edge of your seat.

The Marriage of Figaro, like *The Magic Flute*, operates on two levels, with two love stories, against a background of latent social revolution. A contemporary opera in 1786, all the action takes place in one day of an aristocrat's household, and the music and story portray very real characters. It is a brilliant opera, with music of exceptional beauty and variety. The hero Figaro's subversive *Se vuol ballare, signor contino* (If you would dance, my pretty Count), the Countess's infinitely sad *Porgi amor* (Grant me love), the pageboy Cherubino's *Parlo d'amor* (I speak of love), are just three of the great arias, and Mozart is at his glorious peak throughout. The poignancy when the errant Count begs his wife's forgiveness, at the climax of the opera, is tear-jerking for any romantic soul. The whole opera is one of the glories of the world, for its combination of music and humanity.

Cosi fan Tutte (All women are the same) also has a contemporary setting, and another provocative subject, infidelity in relationships. For many years *Cosi* was derided by prudes for its perceived immoral content and frivolous theme (Beethoven disapproved, for example), but today it has come into its own for the timeless commentary on human nature, and of course it has music of quite exceptional quality. It exudes a joyous atmosphere that has been described as 'air . . . so soft that one has only to breathe it to be happy.' It is a very fast-moving opera, with few solo arias, and the style is immediately set by the opening trio where Ferrando and Guglielmo rhapsodise about the faithfulness of their fiancées, Dorabella and Fiordiligi, to Don Alfonso – a cynical man of the world. He suggests a test, and the opera is on its way with one lovely number after another.

Mozart wrote other operas in his maturity, and *Il Seraglio* (The Abduction from the Harem) is a delight, even if it is based on a contrived and comical situation. *Idomineo* is great music linked to a typical Greek myth libretto of the time, and thus perhaps a little more difficult to relate to. *La Clemenza di Tito* (The Clemency of Titus), written hurriedly in 1791, is also of this style. A number of operas exist from Mozart's youth, but are seldom heard.

Do remember the opportunity exists for you to get acquainted with operas via excerpts on recordings, although excerpts are inevitably selective and you lose a sense of the whole opera. It also takes a little time to get used to the spoken or sung dialogue between the musical numbers, either in the Italian or German. They are best followed with the text supplied with the recording, for full understanding.

Choral music

Before the famous *Requiem*, Mozart wrote a short choral work – just three minutes long – of unsurpassed beauty. *Ave Verum Corpus* has been described thus by Karl Geiringer: 'rarely has so much fervour and classical beauty been poured into so tiny a vessel.'

The *Great C minor Mass*, K427, is unfinished, like the *Requiem*, but it is written on such a large scale in its four completed sections that it is still a very substantial work. Einstein, an authority on music as well as science, called it 'a magnificent torso'. It shares a restrained classical seriousness with the *Requiem*. The *Kyrie* (Lord) opens in sombre mood which is lightened by the entry of the soprano soloist. The *Gloria* switches to an exultant mood, with trumpets prominent. There are vocal gymnastics in the *Laudamus Te* (we praise Thee), but perhaps the most beautiful part is the *Et Incarnatus Est* (and was incarnate), an ethereal experience.

Of Mozart's other choral works, most were written in Salzburg. The *Kyrie in D minor*, K341, is a slender masterpiece with marvellous and prominent horn parts, an exultant work. Other attractive works include the *Coronation Mass*, K317.

Other concertos

Mozart's other concertos include some great favourites. Horn soloists would be lost without the four *Horn Concertos* that Mozart wrote for his friend Ignaz Leutgeb. They are enormous fun, and the French horn has an evocative, mellow tone, nowhere better displayed than in these works. The finale of the last concerto has the famous hunting theme. The *Clarinet Concerto*, written in his last months, is an elegiac work, written for a favourite instrument and a virtuoso performer, Anton Stadler. This beautifully crafted concerto seems ideally suited to late night listening, when the stillness matches the concerto's tranquillity.

A longer and serious masterpiece is the *Sinfonia Concertante for Violin and Viola*, K364. Essentially a concerto for two instruments, it represents the flowering of Mozart into his full maturity. The interplay between the two solo instruments is matched by that of the strings in the orchestra. There is great nobility in the first movement, but the mood swings between several emotions. The slow movement is profound, helped by the mellow sound of the viola. Together with its partner, the violin, you have two instruments in glorious harmony. The finale is happy and jaunty. This work should be ranked amongst the great concertos for violin.

Mozart composed five violin concertos in 1775 for the leader of the Salzburg orchestra, Brunetti. They are attractive early works, of which the *Third*, *Fourth* and *Fifth* are the best. Try the *Fifth*, with its ravishing second theme in the opening, and the music in the Turkish style that is injected into the finale.

Mozart also wrote highly enjoyable concertos for bassoon, flute (two), and oboe, as well as two more sinfonia concertante, for flute and harp, and for four wind instruments.

Chamber music

There is a great wealth of chamber music for those who like the more intimate experience of music for a few instruments. The *Quintet for Piano and Winds*, K452, was considered by Mozart to be his best composition at the time, and it has a marvellous richness, both in themes and the sound of the rare combination of instruments.

The intimacy of Mozart's writing for small ensembles is also beautifully displayed in his *Clarinet Quintet*. Like the *Clarinet Concerto*, I find it to be ideal late night music. A string quartet ushers in the clarinet to a wistful theme, and this mood prevails throughout the first movement. The clarinet leads a rapt slow movement of tender musings. The mood starts to brighten in the minuet, and the last movement contains an attractive set of variations, where exuberance ultimately prevails, touched by nostalgia.

The two *Piano Quartets* are mature masterpieces for piano, violin, viola and cello. The *First* is in Mozart's serious key of G minor, and opens with an assertive and rhythmic statement. It is full of felicitous touches, and has a moving slow movement. The *Second Piano Quartet* sounds a little like a piano concerto without the orchestra. It is in the happy key of E flat, and opens with great confidence. The lyrical first movement is followed by a serene slow movement, similar in style to some of the piano concertos, the finale is a cheerful, jaunty culmination.

The string chamber music has much to offer, but I would particularly recommend that you try:

– the *Divertimento for String Trio* (K563) which is long (about forty minutes) but contains fantastic music. The last of the six movements has one of those instantly memorable themes, of sublime simplicity, that can haunt you.

– The *String Quartet No.19*, known as the *Dissonance* because of its stark introduction, develops an urgent first movement, with rich melodies and some exquisite touches, such as the gentle ending. These qualities continue in the song-like and reflective slow movement. The minuet is followed by an appealing and fast-moving finale.

– The *String Quintet No. 4* (K516), is a work imbued in the first movement with the same spirit as *Symphony No.40*, and is in the same G minor key. The minuet comes second for a change, but it is the adagio that is the gem, an occasionally interrupted rhapsody. The originality continues with an innovative introduction to the last movement before it bursts into an attractive and lively allegro.

You can take it that any of Mozart's last ten string quartets, and the other mature string quintets, are inspired. Whether you get to know them will depends on whether you are, or become, a chamber music fan, or a total Mozart fan.

Serenades

Half way in scale between chamber music and the symphonies lie Mozart's thirteen serenades. The famous *Eine Kleine Nachtmusik*, the last serenade, is about as perfect as a piece of music can be, as exquisite as it is striking.

The *Wind Serenades* (Nos.10–12) are like some of the interludes for winds in the last piano concertos, absolutely delectable with their blend of instruments. The first of these is the best known, although the longest. If you saw 'Amadeus' you will remember Salieri, in his first experience of Mozart's music, in ecstasy as the oboe introduced the main theme of the adagio with supreme poignancy.

Of the other serenades, the *Haffner* – written for the marriage of the burgomaster of Salzberg's daughter, Elizabeth Haffner, in 1776 – is best known, a large scale and happy work. But in this type of music, and the very similar ones called divertimenti, Mozart is never less than outstanding value.

Piano music

Mozart wrote 18 piano sonatas, and many other piano pieces. They are amongst his most under-appreciated works by the public in general, without the perceived individuality and marketing advantage of Beethoven's named sonatas (e.g. Moonlight). Begin with *No.14* in the key of C minor, which seems very close to Beethoven in the first movement. Drama and energy are married to a powerful theme to great effect. A reflective slow movement contains some entrancing passages that would melt a heart of stone. The finale combines contemplation and fireworks in equal and contrasting measure.

Mozart wrote great music in forms not covered here – for example: concert arias for voice and orchestra; violin sonatas: and piano trios. But the music described above covers enough masterpieces to take you a long way.

Ludwig van Beethoven

4

BEETHOVEN

Beethoven *His Life*

*L*udwig van Beethoven was born on December 15, 1770, in Bonn, Germany. His family were musicians to the Elector of Cologne, his father Johann being a court tenor and teacher. His grandfather, also called Ludwig, was Kapellmeister, and therefore his grandson could reasonably be expected to follow the family tradition and become a musician. His mother, Maria, came from a poor family of servants to the Elector.

Beethoven was the eldest of three surviving children, four others having died soon after birth or in early infancy. His brothers Caspar and Nikolaus were born in 1774 and 1776. Grandfather Ludwig died in 1773, and Beethoven's father increasingly took to drink. The boy was brought up in very trying home circumstances, and his father was a very harsh music teacher, who used to beat him regularly.

In spite of the hard regime, Beethoven showed a natural talent for music, particularly on the clavier. He reputedly gave his first public recital at the age of seven, and after this his father sought out better qualified teachers for him. He was lucky that an outstanding musician, Christian Neefe, settled in Bonn in 1779, and took the young Beethoven under his wing.

Beethoven gave up school for a career in music at the age of 11, and was soon acting as Neefe's deputy, playing the harpsichord and organ in the Elector's Court. Neefe wrote that Beethoven 'would surely become a second Wolfgang Mozart were he to continue as he has begun.' By now, Beethoven was writing his first compositions.

His teenage years were difficult due to the situation at home. A young brother died, and his father's drink problem grew worse. Neefe persuaded the Elector that Beethoven should go to Vienna to take lessons from Mozart, and at the same time get some respite from the home pressures.

Beethoven's trip to Vienna in 1787 was sadly cut short because his mother was dying of consumption, and he had to return home after only two weeks. It is a nice story that during this time Beethoven played for Mozart, and Mozart's comment was 'keep an eye on this young man: some day he will give the world something to talk about' but it is not proven that they actually met, or that, if they did, Beethoven received any lessons from him. Soon after his return to Bonn, Beethoven's mother died and he effectively became head of his family at the age of 17. His young sister died a few months later to add to his sorrows, and to manage the family finances he petitioned the Elector to receive half his father's salary. He was well-established at the Court, played the viola in the Opera orchestra, and made some good friends in high places. He also gained first hand experience of Mozart's operas.

Beethoven composed two large scale cantatas (choral works) in 1790 to commemorate first the death of Emperor Joseph II and then the accession of Emperor Leopold. His reputation for improvising on the piano was exceptional, and he must have met Joseph Haydn in that year, as the great man visited the Elector's Court on his way to London.

It was on Haydn's return two years later that he was shown some of Beethoven's work and he agreed to take on the budding composer as his pupil in Vienna. Beethoven arrived there in November, with an introduction from Count Waldstein which was to open many doors for him. The Count had written in farewell: 'with the help of assiduous labour you shall receive Mozart's spirit from Haydn's hands'. Beethoven's father died in the following month and the composer never returned to his birthplace.

Beethoven soon made an impact on Viennese musical life. He rapidly became the leading piano virtuoso of the 1790's, taking the place Mozart had occupied during the previous decade. Like Mozart, he was well accepted by the aristocracy, and developed many friends amongst them. A number are still remembered today because Beethoven dedicated compositions to them.

His main patron was Prince Lichnowsky, and after initially living in the same building as the Prince, he moved in with the household for several years, and the Prince and Princess became his close friends.

Beethoven was independently minded, like Mozart, and developed a reputation for stubbornness and a strong will. He played the piano at the salons only when he felt inclined, and was regarded as a 'difficult genius'.

Beethoven was primarily a virtuoso pianist and extemporiser during his early Viennese years. Composition was a slowly gathered gift, and his first significant works weren't composed until 1795. Naturally, these works were for piano, the first sonatas and concertos. Whilst Beethoven studied under Haydn and other composers, he did this simply to acquire the art of composition. He was very much his own man, and didn't want to be seen as anyone's pupil.

Surprisingly, he didn't appear in an official concert until March 1795, when he gave performances on three consecutive nights. From this time on he was the hero of musical Vienna, and in the traditional virtuoso competitions against visiting pianists he remained supreme. More importantly, he found little difficulty in securing a publisher for his new works.

The last few years of the 18th century were developmental ones for Beethoven, and not marked by great events for him. His two brothers had left Bonn for Vienna. He had numerous affairs of the heart, although he was to remain a bachelor all his life. Somehow one senses that Beethoven's music would not have been the same if he had found marital bliss.

1800 saw the emergence of the fully mature composer. Beethoven gave a benefit concert on April 2 which included his new *First Symphony*, the revised *First Piano Concerto*, and the new, and excellent, *Septet* for four stringed and three wind instruments. Here at last was Mozart's successor! With an enlightened patron, Prince Lichnowsky, settling a reasonable income on him, everything seemed set fair.

But with the sort of tragedy that cut Mozart down, and was to do the same to Schubert in due course, Beethoven's life was about to be shattered. For a musician, deafness is a kind of death, and for some time Beethoven had been aware of a gradual falling off in his hearing. Everything would change, the ability to perform, the ability to communicate, and perhaps the ability to compose. Professional and social death, just at the start of his full flowering.

35

Beethoven first confided his fears to his closest friends in 1801. In fact, deafness was to creep up steadily over many years, and it was not to be just the silence of deafness, 'my ears continue to hum and buzz day and night'. It was a desperate man who went off to the village of Heiligenstadt in the summer of the next year. Here he wrote the famous 'Heiligenstadt Testament' which includes the following passages.

> *O my fellow men, who consider me or describe me as unfriendly, peevish or even misanthropic, how greatly do you wrong me. For you do not know the secret reason why I appear to you to be so.*

> *Yet I could not bring myself to say to people: 'Speak up, shout, for I am deaf'. Alas! how could I possibly refer to the impairing of a sense which in me should be more perfectly developed than in other people.*

> *But how humiliated I have felt if somebody standing beside me heard the sound of a flute in the distance and I heard nothing.*

> *I was on the point of putting an end to my life – the only thing that held me back was my art. For indeed it seemed impossible for me to leave this world before producing all the works that I felt the urge to compose.*

The Heiligenstadt crisis set Beethoven onto a higher plane of creation. In coming to terms with his deafness he embarked on what is often referred to as his 'heroic' period. The *Third Symphony*, (the *Sinfonia Eroica*) written in 1803, is arguably the greatest ever written, and of a scale and power unprecedented for its time. In Beethoven's mind the symphony was entitled '*Bonaparte*', as Napoleon was the current republican hero of much of Europe, and represented ideals close to Beethoven's heart. But when Napoleon declared himself Emperor, he lost both Beethoven's support and the dedication of the symphony.

Beethoven composed some of the world's most famous music in the next six years, when he was at his most creative. During this time he was also industriously building up his international reputation and his earnings, wrestling with his opera, *Leonora*, and romancing the Countess Josephine Deym (one of his pupils). These were dramatic years, when Vienna was caught up in war and in 1805 was under French occupation.

The *Eroica* was given its first performance early in 1805, but **the** concert of Beethoven's heroic period was the one given at the Theater an der Wien on December 22 in 1808, which saw the premieres of the

Fifth and *Sixth Symphonies*, the *Fourth Piano Concerto*, and the *Choral Fantasia*. Around this time Beethoven was offered a secure position outside Austria, and he used this to negotiate a guaranteed income in Vienna from the Emperor's youngest brother, the Archduke Rudolph (a pupil of his), and other members of the aristocracy.

Beethoven's highly productive phase lasted for ten years: though his deafness had now reached the point where he could no longer perform effectively as a soloist, his position as a celebrity was unique. In 1812 he met the great German poet Goethe who commented; 'His talent amazed me, but he is an utterly untamed personality, who is not altogether wrong in holding the world to be detestable.' This year saw the completion of two outstanding symphonies, the *Seventh* and *Eighth*.

1813 saw Beethoven in crisis again, deeply depressed by the ending of his deepest emotional relationship. The identity of the 'Immortal Beloved', so referred to in an unsent letter discovered after Beethoven's death, was only recently proved beyond reasonable doubt. Antonie Brentano was married, and clearly Beethoven was 'in love'. It was another of Beethoven's unattainable relationships. Contributing to his difficulties were the death of one of his benefactors and the effects of rampant inflation on his already diminished income.

The next years were not gratifying ones, as Beethoven's behaviour became increasingly erratic. He dressed in a slovenly way and his apartment was like a pig-sty. His output dropped dramatically, both in terms of quantity and quality, with the exception of the successful revision of his opera, renamed *Fidelio*.

But the best example of his strange frame of mind was his determination to get custody of his nephew, the son of his recently deceased brother, Caspar, in 1815. Beethoven was obviously unsuited to bringing up a nine-year-old, but was unremitting in his efforts to achieve custody rather than leave the boy with his mother. No doubt psychologists could shed light on this, but the fact is that the unseemly wrangling lasted for five years at the cost of his composing. During these years his output was extremely limited.

By the end of 1818, Beethoven's batteries were recharging, and he was ready to enter the last, and greatest, phase of his life as a composer. He had already moved in a new direction in a few recently composed works, and his remaining compositions were typically to be more concentrated, more powerful, more spiritual and intellectual than before.

Increasingly Beethoven was seen as a 'mad genius', and his new composing style was appreciated by few. He would walk through the streets of Vienna, shabbily dressed, his gestures and comments attracting attention and comment. But his friends were true and still venerated him.

His great Mass, the *Missa Solemnis*, was completed in 1823, to be followed by the *Ninth Symphony*, and he returned to writing string quartets after receiving a commission from a Russian prince. These 'late' quartets have become the most celebrated works in this form, although they were considered too modern for many years. Beethoven now had more commissions than he could possibly cope with, and the fees were generous.

The last great concert in Beethoven's lifetime premiering his works took place on May 7, 1824, when the *Ninth Symphony* and three sections of the *Missa Solemnis* were given. The theatre was full, and the applause overwhelming. After the symphony, Beethoven had to be turned round to see the acclaim which he could no longer hear.

Problems with his nephew recurred in 1826, when Karl tried to shoot himself. He was then enlisted as a cadet in the army, and Beethoven's unfortunate essay into child rearing was over. When the two of them were returning to Vienna from a trip in December of that year, however, Beethoven caught a chill which developed into pneumonia. His financial situation during his illness was helped enormously by a gift of a hundred pounds from the Philharmonic Society in London, but his condition grew worse.

He was operated on twice to remove abdominal fluids, but it was clear he was dying, and his friends gathered around him during the last weeks. He fell into a coma on March 24, and late in the afternoon of the 26th, with a thunderstorm raging and snow falling, he opened his eyes, raised his right arm and clenched his fist. It dropped back and Beethoven was dead.

Three days later, 20,000 thousand people turned out for his funeral procession. This time the Viennese understood that a great man and musician had died.

Beethoven *The Person*

Beethoven was about 5ft.4ins tall, with a dark and swarthy appearance, and was considered Spanish-looking in his youth. He was a very strong-minded person, and an independent thinker. A staunch republican, he regarded himself equal to royalty, but more fundamentally, he considered all men to be equal.

He liked to show his independence, and whilst he had the social graces to be accepted fully by Viennese society, he could also be quite boorish, sometimes behaving like a temperamental prima donna and refusing to perform. The aristocracy tolerated his behaviour, and many of the women found him fascinating.

Beethoven was a romantic idealist, and frequently in love, though his writings on his state of mind and emotions sometimes show a melodramatic tendency. Probably as a result of his drunken father's appalling behaviour, he tended to put women on a pedestal, as he had done his mother, and preferred to keep them there, safely at a distance. He would probably have run a mile if the right woman had consented to marry him!

To become deaf in his thirties was a terrible blow, and led him towards a somewhat reclusive life. He bore this tragedy with great fortitude, but became increasingly slovenly over time, in both his dress and his personal habits. He behaved as though he were ostracised and not part of society.

He was pretty mixed up psychologically in his attitude to his family. His attempts to adopt his nephew Karl were unhealthy and selfish, as demonstrated by Karl's suicide attempt.

In spite of his considerable eccentricity, and a somewhat prickly side, he was basically good-natured and inspired love, reverence, and loyalty from his inner circle.

Beethoven *His Music*

Beethoven had a superbly positive outlook. His output contains a very high proportion of uplifting works, and where tragedy does enter, as in the second movement of the *Eroica Symphony*, it is overtaken by the music that follows. It is argued that the reason why Mozart has over-taken Beethoven as the most popular composer is that the simple tri-umph of good over evil, which Beethoven can so wonderfully convey, is thought less appropriate today than the wider subtleties of human emotions, in particular sadness and cynicism, contained in Mozart.

Beethoven comes over very strongly, and the power of his music makes him the favourite for many newcomers to classical music. His main groups of compositions are:

– Symphonies: nine, all regularly played.

– Concertos: five for piano, one for violin, and one for piano, violin, and cello.

– Piano Sonatas: a marvellous series of 32.

– Chamber music: 16 string quartets plus other great works for piano trio, cello and piano, and violin and piano.

In addition, Beethoven composed magnificent works for many other settings, of which his opera, *Fidelio*, and the *Missa Solemnis* stand out.

For the 'Beethoven Starterpack' I suggest you approach the following different aspects of this heroic composer:

1 Symphonies The *Fifth Symphony* is a most powerful and concise work, totally unlike any other symphony written up to that time. Built on the famous rhythm pa-pa-pa-Paa (which has been described as Fate knocking at the door), the first movement is highly dramatic, and over in a flash in a good performance. It also gives a clear demonstration of a major characteristic of Beethoven in many of his works – a powerful, 'masculine', first theme that is followed by a contrasting, soft, 'feminine' second theme. The most memorable part of this symphony is the tran-sition from the third to the last movement. The highly original scherzo, with its lumbering double basses, descends into a mysterious near-silence, from which gradually erupts a full orchestral crescendo, and then the trumpets, horns and trombones (the latter making their first appearance in a major composer's symphony) blaze into a triumphant and exalting C major theme.

2 Piano concertos The *Fifth Piano Concerto*, nicknamed the *Emperor* because it is an imperious work, is spell-binding right from the initial powerful chords. The piano and orchestra are formidable opponents for much of the first movement, but the second is a rapt and beautiful dialogue between the two. It leads magically, without a break, into a swinging finale.

3 The Violin Concerto Never mind about this being another concerto, it is such an obviously beautiful composition that it is an ideal introductory piece. Opening with five gentle timpani notes, its orchestral introduction displays themes conveying an unsurpassed purity, nobility, and yearning. The violin, such an expressive instrument, is perfectly suited to this music. The first movement is inspirational, the second a beautiful adagio, the third movement an exhilarating end to this glorious work.

4 Piano Sonatas The *Moonlight Sonata*, with its serene, simple, and famous opening movement, is a very seductive entry into the marvellous piano sonatas. A highly romantic work, in recordings it is typically grouped with two out of three of the *Pathetique*, *Waldstein* and *Appassionata* sonatas. These are all amongst the greatest works in the piano repertoire, and are easily approachable, being exciting and rich in great themes (see below).

5 Chamber music The *Archduke Trio* for piano, violin, and cello, is a very lyrical work, its beauty lying not only in the themes, but in the conversations between the instruments. It opens with a theme of majestic self-confidence. The second movement, a lilting scherzo, is followed by one of Beethoven's great and moving slow movements, which in turn runs directly into a jaunty finale.

These works will give you the essence of Beethoven, and although he wrote less than Mozart, there are still dozens of works for you to get to know. Those composed in his last years offer particular depth and profundity, as Beethoven continued to develop as a composer right to the end of his life.

Symphonies

No composer's symphonies display such a variety of character as Beethoven's. The so-called odd-number symphonies (3,5,7,9) are seen as displaying his powerful side, but they are all an essential part of a collection of classical music.

No. 3 Eroica This great symphony was a considerable shock to the audience at its premiere because of the intensity and power of the first movement, the funeral march that followed, and the symphony's unprecedented length (about 50 minutes). From the two magnificent opening chords, the music is on a mighty and heroic scale, but humour is there too. The following funeral march conveys great loss and tragedy, lightened briefly by a poignant interlude of solace. A scherzo with horns strident leads into a set of variations on a humorous theme, which belies the symphony's title. Beethoven finishes the variations with one of great beauty, leading into a magisterial and exhilarating ending.

No. 6 Pastoral Beethoven intended to convey the feelings of being in the countryside in this unique symphony, and he totally succeeded. It is a true celebration of nature, and a radiant and therapeutic experience. The movements are described as: 1. *Awakening of happy feelings on arriving in the country*; 2. *By the brook*; 3. *Joyous gathering of country folk*; 4. *Storm*; 5. *Shepherd's song, happy and thankful feelings after the storm*. This is a glorious and very popular work, capped by the final hymn of thanksgiving. It tells us quite a lot about Beethoven the man, as well.

No. 7 Described by the great operatic composer Richard Wagner as the apotheosis of the dance, the Seventh has enormous rhythmic vitality. A slow and powerful introduction leads into a swirling allegro, with strings and horns dominant. The second movement, melancholic and emotionally charged, is followed by a marvellous scherzo that really swings, over an insistent rhythm. Driving and persistent rhythms propel the finale to a majestic climax where the horns take the honours.

No. 9 Choral Once thought to be the aberration in Beethoven's symphonic cycle, it has now come into its own. The famous *Ode to Joy* last movement is truly thrilling, with a chorus and soloists joining the orchestra for the first time in a symphony. The first movement has great power and concentration, the scherzo is like a celestial clock, and the third movement is Beethoven's most sublime adagio.

No. 8 Shorter than the other mature Beethoven symphonies, it is relatively, and unjustly, neglected. The first movement has marvellous momentum and builds to a thrilling climax, the second – a tribute to the inventor of the metronome – ticks along merrily. An unusual minuet, much stronger than the style of Mozart or Haydn, is followed by a fizzing finale. Great music, with a lot of humour.

No. 4 A superb classical, rather than romantic, work which again suffers under the shadow of its popular companions. It opens with a stately adagio, which winds up into a lively allegro. This is no lightweight work, though! A lovely slow movement, a bubbly scherzo, and the symphony finishes with a rollicking and humorous finale. The symphony gives the sense that all the sections of the orchestra are having a great time as they toss the themes around.

No. 2 A work of considerable strength, with Beethoven showing masterly use of all the different voices in the orchestra. The slow movement is inspired, and a forerunner of that in the Ninth Symphony.

No. 1 Still very much in the Haydn tradition in scale and content, this thoroughly enjoyable symphony has the clear Beethoven vitality and humour.

Concertos

The *Fourth Piano Concerto* is an equal partner to the *Emperor*, although very different in mood. Instead of the majestic chords for piano and orchestra, we have the piano entering alone with a gentle and simple theme which is then taken up by the orchestra. This first movement is one of Beethoven's loveliest creations, and some recordings include a cadenza (solo display part) which is said to best represent what Beethoven's own improvisations were like. (Stunning, with a great cascade of notes!) The slow movement sees the piano gradually taming a fierce orchestra, another stroke of great originality, and the effect is magical. The last movement is less remarkable but nicely rounds off this pearl of a concerto.

The *Third Piano Concerto*, like the *First*, is written in the traditional classical style. Composed mainly in the sombre key of C minor, it alternates the strong and the lyrical in the first movement. The slow movement, moving into a happier major key, offers gentle musings between the piano and orchestra, with a strong emotional undercurrent. The last movement returns to C minor, but bursts into an exciting presto to end in happy C major.

The *First Piano Concerto* (actually written second) is a delightful work and not to be missed. Its happy mood is immediately set by the orchestral introduction, the second theme being a delicate beauty. The slow movement is radiant, intimate musings from the piano are accompanied by orchestral caresses, and then the last movement (which can seem the least strong in Beethoven's concertos) provides a sparkling contrast as it rushes brilliantly along.

The *Second Piano Concerto* is enjoyable without having, understandably, quite the strength of character of its successors. All the Beethovenian features are in evidence, and the slow movement is passionate and moving.

The *Triple Concerto* has the piano, violin, and cello, as its solo instruments. It opens gently and builds into a theme with a marvellous swagger, Beethoven in his best relaxed form. It keeps to a chamber style rather than the grand heroic manner, a piano trio with orchestra. The cello plays a prominent part in the lyrical slow movement, where the soloists have a hushed orchestra, and they lead straight into the rumbustuous, playful last movement of this neglected work.

Piano sonatas

There isn't one sonata in the 32 that doesn't have its own character, nor one that is not worth knowing. And amongst them are the greatest piano sonatas ever written, and moving slow movements – where Beethoven is supreme – abound. Many of the sonatas are instantly enjoyable, hence a rather large selection.

No. 3 A happy work, including a first movement with instantly memorable melodies, a profound adagio for a slow movement, and a very catchy finale.

No. 4 This sonata has great tunes and pianistic effects in its first movement, and an intense slow movement. The third movement has a lilting theme, and the work concludes with a rondo – a movement with a theme that comes round several times – which starts gently but rises in dramatic intensity before dying away.

No. 8 Pathetique A serious introduction and the C minor key herald Beethoven's first masterpiece. It leads to a dramatic and rushing allegro which switches into a slower, but spritely, theme. The flowing adagio is one of his most beautiful and famous, absolutely melting. The last movement is short, and in less serious vein.

No. 15 Pastoral A splendidly relaxing, but quite ardent opening movement is followed by an andante that was one of Beethoven's favourite slow movements. A fleeting scherzo and then the last movement brings a return of the relaxed, serene mood again. This time he alternates the lyricism with dynamism, and the movement finishes in an exciting presto.

No. 17 The Tempest A powerful first movement, in a pre-dominantly agitated mood, an adagio which is restless, and a lilting but powerful finale make up this sonata.

No. 18 A first movement of great delicacy for Beethoven is followed by a marvellous, lively, second movement and a gracious slow minuet. A presto of great fun and some very catchy tunes rounds off this marvellous work.

No. 21 Waldstein One of the greatest piano sonatas, it is an incandescent work. The first movement races along for most of the time, with soaring tunes and fantastic fingerwork producing cascades of notes. A short and searching adagio serves as an introduction to the glorious finale which builds inexorably to a virtuoso climax.

No. 23 Appassionata An equal partner to the *Waldstein*, it opens mysteriously before the introduction of a rhythmic second theme, after which the first movement is propelled along, with strength visited regularly by gentleness. A beautiful adagio of great simplicity, that would melt a heart of stone, leads into a powerful allegro.

No. 25 This has to be a favourite, launching at a fast tempo into some very catchy themes, developed with genius and much wit. A flowing slow movement is followed by a very lively and melodic finale – all in less than ten minutes!

In the guidebook, 'The Beethoven Companion', Philip Barford aptly describes the last five sonatas as 'overwhelming in effect, tremendous in musical substance, and profound in psycho-spiritual depth'. They do require repeated hearings and familiarity with the preceding sonatas, to appreciate them fully, but they can be easily approached on disc. Try them, see if you like them, but don't rush. The same applies to Beethoven's last major piano work, his *33 Variations on a Waltz by Diabelli*. After trying the most popular sonatas, if you find you take to these works, you should seriously consider buying a complete set of the sonatas. The sets are available at remarkably low prices and you will avoid duplication and save money in the long run, apart from having a fabulous experience close at hand.

Other works

The opera *Fidelio* was a long time arriving at its final form, but it is a masterpiece. It is the tale of the rescue of a man (Florestan) from prison by his wife (Leonora) – the triumph of good over evil, and of the power of marital love. It is superb Beethoven: the effect in the first act when the fellow prisoners come out of their cells into daylight is emotionally supercharged, but the main action takes place in the second act, in Florestan's cell, and it is spell-binding. High drama, marvellous music, and Florestan is saved by his heroic wife (disguised as a man, Fidelio) at the last moment. In the general rejoicing afterwards, Leonora is given the keys to unlock Florestan's chains, and Beethoven's music is sublime for this supremely poignant scene. The chorus that ends the opera is on a par with the finale of the *Ninth Symphony*, and not unrelated to it.

Beethoven wrote four overtures altogether for *Fidelio*, and numerous other ones, usually for incidental music for plays. *Egmont*, *Prometheus*, *Coriolan*, *The Consecration of the House*, together with *Fidelio* and its three trial companions, *Leonora Nos.1–3*, make up a great set of short Beethoven pieces. *Egmont* and *Leonora No.3* are particularly fine.

The *Missa Solemnis* is at the very peak of settings of the Mass, an overwhelming experience. Beethoven wrote above the score 'From the heart, may it in turn go to the heart'. Each of the seven sections is superb, the opening *Kyrie* sets the scale of power and gentle beauty, before the *Gloria* rushes on the scene, with the chorus in full flight. Two thirds of the way through, at the words *Quoniam tu solus Sanctus* (Only Thou art holy), one of the most exhilarating passages in all music commences. Beethoven builds a great fugue and enormous tension before the final word, 'Gloria', is hurled out by the chorus. The *Credo* (I believe) opens in a mood of exaltation, and also has a glorious fugue for chorus and orchestra. The *Sanctus* (Holy) offers a quieter movement with a sublime solo violin passage representing the Holy Spirit descending, and the Mass ends with the *Agnus Dei* (Lamb of God), and the fervent plea *Dona Nobis Pacem* (Give us peace), after threatening passages from trumpets and drums.

The *C major Mass* would be much better known if it weren't for its big brother. It is a masterly work on a more mortal level than the *Missa Solemnis* – pure middle-period Beethoven, from its lovely opening Kyrie to the stroke of genius that completes the work with the final *Dona Nobis Pacem* and the return of the opening theme.

The *Choral Fantasia* for piano, chorus, and orchestra is an unusual work, quite short, but very striking. Its main theme is a forerunner of the *Ode to Joy* in the last movement of the *Ninth Symphony*. The *Fantasia* begins with an extended piano solo, before the orchestra joins in, to be later followed by the chorus.

Chamber music

Beethoven wrote much outstanding chamber music for a wide variety of instrumental combinations. Here are the some of the high spots.

Violin sonatas (Piano and Violin). Beethoven wrote ten works of which *No.10* is the greatest, with one of his great lyrical themes in the first movement, a pensive adagio which runs into a scherzo of bouncy rhythm and a gentle waltz in its middle section. The sonata is concluded by a set of variations of widely swinging moods based on an irresistable theme. The two sonatas with titles, *No.5 Spring* and *No.9 Kreutzer*, are attractive and popular follow up works.

Cello sonatas (Cello and piano). Beethoven wrote five cello sonatas, an innovatory combination at the time. The essential listening is the *Third*. An expansive theme is introduced quietly by the cello, and then the piano joins in. The mood soon quickens to create a powerful and very appealing movement. A perky scherzo is followed by a briefly intense and beautiful slow passage, hardly a slow movement, which quickly accelerates into a finale that swings along to an attractive and lively theme.

Beethoven's 16 string quartets cover his entire composing career. Like his piano sonatas, there is not one that can be discounted. They split themselves into groups equating to Beethoven's so-called 'Early', 'Middle', and 'Late' periods; *Nos.1–6*, *7–11*, and *12–16* respectively. Held in awe by many, including outstanding musicians, the late quartets are like their counterparts, the last piano sonatas, in having great depth, but differ, in my view, in being more likely to be attractive to the newcomer who finds that he or she likes the particular musical medium.

No.15 has a slow movement of extraordinary beauty and intensity. This movement, the third, is entitled *Hymn of gratitude from a convalescent to the Divinity in the Lydian mode*. About 20 minutes long, it is a hypnotic experience, try listening to it late at night with just candlelight. The other four movements provide a strong setting for this jewel.

If this music gets to you, you may choose to try the other late quartets. *No.12* starts with majestic chords at a slow tempo, and then launches into an expansive allegro. The opening returns to impressive effect during the movement. The slow movement is a set of variations providing great variety of mood, from introspection to playfulness. It is a less intense sister to the adagio in *No.15*. A craggy scherzo and striking finale complete a work that was revolutionary in its time.

A path from these quartets would perhaps go to *Nos.13* and *14* (both on the same large scale) followed by *No.16*, and then work backwards through the other quartets.

If you don't take to the late quartets, there is another route into Beethoven's chamber music for strings. The *String Quintet* is a very accessible work to be tried independently from the string quartets. A graceful theme with a pulsating accompaniment draws you into an instantly appealing movement. The relaxed mood continues in a captivating adagio, but urgency enters with the scherzo and remains throughout the gripping finale. If you like this quintet, you might then try the early quartets.

Beethoven's *Septet* was one of his early successes, and is an attractive and approachable work, bridging the gap between Mozart and Beethoven's later compositions. Scored for four string instruments and three winds – a combination that sounds superb – the slow introduction leads into a delectable and fast-running theme, which sets the mood for an enchanting and happy work. The highspots amongst the remaining five movements are the beautiful and introspective adagio, and the delightful and bubbling presto finale.

The *Quintet for Piano and Winds* is another excellent early work, usually coupled in recordings with its counterpart by Mozart. The combination of instruments is, again, very appealing, and the Quintet is confident and relaxed in the first movement, with typical Beethoven dramatic touches over some great melodies. The slow movement is marked 'andante cantabile', and flowing and singing it certainly is. The finale is jaunty and humorous.

5

BACH

Bach *His Life*

Johann Sebastian Bach was born on March 21, 1685, in Eisenach, Germany. He was the youngest of eight children, of whom four survived infancy. His father, Johann Ambrosius, was the town musician and organist. The Bach family was prolific, intensely musical, religious, closely knit, and spread over many towns.

Bach would have experienced a comprehensive musical education from an early age. The music in church was provided by a highly gifted cousin, Johann Christoph, and his father, emphasizing the family tradition. Bach's mother died when he was nine, his father a year later, and he and his brother were taken in by the recently married eldest brother, also named Johann Christoph, who was organist in a small town called Ohrdruf.

Bach remained in Ohrdruf for five years, learning much from his elder brother, who had been taught first by their father, and then by the organist and composer Pachelbel. Bach was extremely intelligent, determined, and showed tremendous musical potential.

At the age of 15, Bach left Ohrdruf to join the choir at St. Michael's Church in Lüneburg, two hundred miles away. St. Michael's had a large collection of music manuscripts, and Bach heard and performed much great music during his time there, as well as receiving a good education. He travelled widely to enrich his musical experience, focusing on the organ, and in the process developing a considerable expertise in organ construction.

In 1703, Bach was appointed organist at Arnstadt, after demonstrating his virtuoso skills on the new organ at the Neue Kirche. He was well paid, but his time at Arnstadt was occasionally fraught. He was involved in a sword-fight with a member of his choir; he took three months unapproved leave of absence to visit the great organist and composer

Joh. Sebast. Bach.

Buxtehude who lived many miles away in Lübeck and he was reproved for his liberties on the organ during church services. He quickly developed a reputation as an unconventional, brilliant, difficult and independently-minded young man and his future in Armstadt was clearly going to be limited.

However, he did fall in love, with a second cousin of his own age, Maria Barbara Bach, preferring love to the suggested opportunity for becoming Buxtehude's successor by marrying his 30-year-old daughter.

Bach became organist at St. Blasius', Muhlhausen, in 1707, after some family string-pulling and another virtuoso trial recital for the congregation: a cousin succeeded him at Arnstadt in a further example of the Bach family influence. On October 17, Bach and Maria Barbara were married, the start of Bach's first great marriage partnership.

Within a year, Bach was on the move again (replaced by yet another cousin) this time to the court of the Duke of Weimar, 40 miles away. Duke Wilhelm Ernst was extremely religious, but quite enlightened. He gave full support to Bach, including substantial investment in upgrading the organ. This period in Bach's career was one in which the organ dominated his activities. He travelled throughout Germany as an acclaimed organ virtuoso and composed most of his great works for the instrument at this time.

After a while, Bach was promoted to concertmaster at Weimar, giving him a small orchestra and singers to work with, and a requirement to compose a new cantata every month. This marked a new phase in Bach's development. Life in Weimar was good, his family was expanding (amongst his children he had three musically gifted sons), he had friends, pupils, and money.

The good life at Weimar came to an end in 1717. Bach had annoyed his patron by his relationship with the Duke's nephew, and when the Duke's old Kapellmeister died, Bach, the natural successor, was passed over in favour of the Kapellmeister's son. Bach was not a person to brook this insult. He quickly found a much more supportive patron, at another, much smaller, prince's court at Cöthen.

Duke Wilhelm Ernst refused to release Bach from his post however, and when Bach insisted on leaving the Duke, he had him imprisoned. Bach spent four stubborn weeks in jail before the Duke finally gave up and fired him.

Bach was now able to move to his much more prestigious position, albeit in a smaller court. His patron, Prince Leopold, was nine years younger, and a highly proficient musician and lover of the arts. It was for Leopold that Bach wrote his great solo works for violin and cello. With a well-trained small orchestra, Bach's creativity increased dramatically. Tragically, most of Bach's works of this time have been lost, but the Brandenburg Concertos – so-called because they were dedicated to the Margrave of Brandenburg – are a prime example of his genius with his new orchestra.

The great happiness at Cöthen was suddenly broken by the death of Maria Barbara in 1720, whilst Bach was away with his patron. This personal disaster turned Bach back to church music. He remarried 18 months later, to the 20-year-old Anna Magdalena Wilcken, the daughter of one of the court musicians at Cöthen, and a professional singer in her own right. She was to bear him 13 further children, seven of whom died in infancy.

What remained of the idyll of Cöthen came to an end when Prince Leopold married a non-music-loving princess. Music at the court became less important, and Bach, seeing the writing on the wall, decided to move on. He was appointed Leipzig Thomas Cantor in May 1723, a prestigious position with responsibility for Leipzig's church music, and the teaching of music at St. Thomas' church and school. He was to remain there for the rest of his life.

Composition was a major part of Bach's duties. A new cantata was required each Sunday, and he achieved a phenomenal output of works, at the peak of his creativity. In time, Bach developed a reputation amongst the more perceptive music lovers as a true genius, although the bureaucracy at Leipzig (Bach was responsible to 20 or more councillors) meant that he had his enemies as well. It is not unrealistic to say that Leipzig was relatively unaware that it had one of the greatest composers of all time in its midst. Thus the first performance of Bach's mighty religious work, the *St. Matthew Passion*, on Good Friday in 1729, went over the heads of his councillors, who interfered, where possible, in Bach's musical responsibilities.

By 1730, Bach was feeling particularly frustrated by the inadequacy of the resources given to him. He thought of moving on again, but regained his motivation by directing a 'collegium musicum', a society of amateur and professional musicians who gave informal weekly concerts in a coffee house or outdoors. In addition, a new Rector was appointed at the school, and he was a great admirer of Bach. He also introduced many necessary changes in the accommodation and running of the school. Unfortunately, the Rector left in 1734, to be succeeded by a less appealing academic.

In 1733 Bach petitioned for a title in the Elector of Hanover's court. He presented a *Kyrie* and *Gloria* (later to become the major parts of the mighty B minor Mass) to the Elector, but was unsuccessful. However he persevered, dedicating numerous works for state celebrations, including a torchlight performance of one of his works in Leipzig in 1734, in the presence of the Elector. He finally became Court Composer in 1736.

Bach's grown-up sons were now spreading the family network further. Wilhelm Friedman became organist at Dresden, Carl Philipp Emmanuel became harpsichordist to Prince Frederick in Berlin, and Johann Gottfried became organist at Muhlhausen in 1735. The latter was to give Bach much heartache because of his habit of getting into financial difficulties. He died at a young age in 1739.

Bach was not without his critics. He was accused of writing turgid music, and increasingly in his last years, like Beethoven 80 years later, he composed music that was rarely heard, and appreciated by only a few during his lifetime.

In 1747, Bach visited his son in Potsdam, near Berlin, and attended the court of the very musical King Frederick the Great. 'Old Bach' impressed them all with his keyboard improvisations on the fortepiano and the organ. He was given a theme by Frederick on which to improvise a fugue, and he later developed this into the famous *Musical Offering*.

In the last few years of his life he completed the great *B minor Mass* and worked on *The Art of Fugue*, his massive work for harpsichord. In 1750, his eyesight deteriorated drastically as a result of cataracts, and the treatment he received resulted by April in his total blindness. In July his sight returned briefly, but he suffered a stroke which was followed by a fever. He died at a quarter to nine in the evening of July 28.

Bach was buried three days later in the Johanniskirche in Leipzig, in a grave soon to be forgotten. His widow died in poverty ten years later. In 1950 Bach's remains were removed to the Thomaskirche.

Bach *The Person*

Bach was about 5ft.7ins. tall, well built, with a large head on which he usually wore a wig. He had considerable presence. He was a very strong-minded person, and highly intelligent. Full of self-confidence – if he wanted to do something, he would do it. He organised his life and priorities totally to his own satisfaction, if at all possible.

He was very much a family man, in the tradition of the extensive Bach clan, and took great pride in his many children. He clearly had a very high sexual drive. He was unusually blessed in having successive wives whose characters complemented his own, and allowed the creation of two very successful marriages, providing stability and happiness at home.

He was not an easy person to get on with: he could be crusty, and he had a strong temper. He was also a disciplinarian. His powerful personality meant that he usually got his own way and no-one crossed him lightly. He was apt to make enemies with his intransigence, but his musical gifts made most people tolerate his stubbornness.

Bach was serious about his religion. He was a Lutheran Protestant, and was extraordinarily well read on the subject. He was an astute manager of his finances and always lived well within his means, although quite well off.

Bach *The Music*

I am going to describe only a handful of works written by this famous composer. If you believe, as I do, that music is a voyage of discovery, there are two composers always mentioned as the ultimate destination, Mozart and Bach. There is a lovely story concerning God's favourite composer, the two candidates being Bach and Mozart. The difference might be summarised by the famous saying of one Karl Barth 'It may be that when the angels go about their task praising God, they play only Bach. I am sure, however, that when they are together, en famille, they play Mozart.'

Bach's magnificence can be recognised in a number of easily accessible works. But beyond these lie hundreds more that need patience both in discovery and in acquiring familiarity. Works for solo cello, violin, and harpsichord, with their relatively unremitting sound, are not to everyone's taste, and can be particularly off-putting for people in their early exploration of classical music. Two hundred cantatas, mainly religious works, can have a similarly daunting effect.

Yet it is generally considered that Bach wrote some of his greatest music for these instruments or choral forces, and as a result I see these works as one of the ultimate destinations in the exploration of classical music, though beyond the frontiers of this book.

In the first half of the 18th century, Bach's genius stands out for creating music that is exceptional in its originality, and it can offer much to us in the late 20th century. Again and again in the accessible works descibed below, I come back to the unique timeless quality of the music, its seeming ability to continue playing indefinitely, without boring the listener.

Concertos

The *Brandenburg Concertos* are the bedrock of any music collection – a fundamental recommendation. They represent the peak of musical achievement in the early eighteenth century, an extraordinarily inventive selection that we are lucky to have preserved for us, so nearly were they lost like so much of Bach's music. They contain an enormous wealth of styles and instrumentation and a rare democracy amongst the orchestral voices.

Concerto No.1 The initial impression is one of chamber music with horns prominent. The rich first movement is dominated by one of Bach's timeless themes. The mood created is one of vibrant but organised bustle. The intense adagio second movement is led by an oboe and violin. The third movement has marvellous scoring, with all instruments clearly heard, though the horn and violin have pride of place. The finale is a series of dances, with a lovely and dominant recurrent minuet. Horns are, again, much to the forefront.

Concerto No.2 opens with a marvellous allegro, with trumpet, recorder, oboe and violin as the concertante instruments, prominent in front of the chamber orchestra. Again, it sounds as though the theme could continue indefinitely. A flowing andante is followed by a racing and rhythmic allegro, led by a high trumpet.

Concerto No.3 has a masterly opening movement – quintessential Bach. Rich strings are the only instruments apart from the harpsichord continuo (accompaniment) that tinkles away in the background. The slow movement consists only of two slow chords, running immediately into a fast and brilliant allegro.

Concerto No.4 Two recorders flutter their way through this intricate concerto alongside a virtuoso violin, giving a unique sound colour. A lilting allegro, a graceful andante, and finally a stunning fugue (the instruments setting off at intervals, playing the same theme) make up this ethereal work.

Concerto No.5 Prominent flute, violin and harpsichord characterise this concerto, with the last instrument dominant, turning it at times into a harpsichord concerto. The first movement is gradually taken over by the harpsichord, as the instrument is allowed to move from the traditional accompaniment role into one of dominance, leading to an extended cadenza, or solo. The slow movement is a musing trio for the three leading instruments, and is followed by a finale where the full orchestra gradually re-asserts itself, to restore the balance to that of the opening.

Concerto No.6 The deceptively simple, but glorious, opening theme has an amazingly restful effect, demonstrated by the sense of inevitability at each reappearance. It, again, gives the feeling that it could play and be listened to for ever, music for the gods! The rest of this concerto for strings – but without violins – comprises a moving adagio and a bouncy allegro.

Bach's violin concertos are another essential foundation in music. The *Concerto for Two Violins* is extraordinarily expressive, with a slow movement that has the most exquisite interplay between the two instruments. The theme has considerable poignancy and has found fame in a major film. The *Violin Concerto in E major* has the same feel as the Brandenburgs, that of timeless greatness. The rhythmic first movement is followed by a rich and sombre adagio and a lively allegro. The *Violin Concerto in A minor* is an equal match, the high spot being its throbbing slow movement, a profound experience. These concertos, like the

Brandenburgs, can only be described as glorious, and are an essential part of a classical music collection.

Orchestral suites

Bach's four *Orchestral Suites* were composed for dancing, each Suite consisting of an overture followed by several short movements, designed for an individual style of dance. As such, they are lively and varied. Obviously less profound than the works described above, they are, nonetheless, very attractive compositions and play an important and enjoyable part in familiarisation with Bach's musical style. The most famous selection is the *Air* in the *Third Suite*, falsely immortalised as the *Air on the G string*.

Organ music

Bach's prowess as a composer for the organ must be experienced, and you should start by choosing a selection of the most famous pieces. Such a selection will inevitably include the *Toccata and Fugue in D minor*, but there is a host of other works that would justify inclusion. Luckily, Bach's organ music is well represented on disc, and you can explore it easily.

Choral music

For an introduction to Bach's great choral works, the *Magnificat* is ideal. A work of joyous exaltation, it starts with a superb choral movement. It has 11 short sections of considerable variety, and of great beauty. The work ends in triumph, with trumpets blazing.

Bach's greatest choral work, which is ranked alongside Beethoven's *Missa Solemnis*, is the *B minor Mass*. It is easy to be put off by its length – it lasts nearly two hours in performance – but it is one of those works which has instantly enjoyable sections, as well as ones that quickly grow on you, and others that require time to appreciate. It is probably the key to a discovery of the marvels of the great host of Bach's relatively unknown cantatas. There are many sections in the *Mass*, and the opening *Kyrie* sets the mood of worship. The *Gloria* opens in punchy style, fierce rhythms dominating, and it ends with the exalting *Cum Sancto Spiritu in gloria Dei Patris* (With the Holy Ghost in the glory of God). In the

Credo, the concluding chorus *Et Exspecto Resurrectionem mortuorum* (And I look for the Resurrection of the dead) stands out in a similar light, and has marvellous interplay between the choral voices – sopranos, contraltos, tenors and basses – with a joyful theme. The mood of spiritual transcendence continues into the *Sanctus* (Holy), before retreating and then swelling to a fervent prayer for peace. The inspiration of this music shines strongly.

The other Bach choral work rightly acclaimed as one of the masterpieces in all music is the *St. Matthew Passion*. Half as long again as the *B minor Mass*, it depicts in music the story of Christ's arrest, trial, crucifixion and burial. From the ardent opening chorus, Bach provides inspired music suited to his text. The drama is unfolded with a narrative, solo parts for the main characters, and choruses. With patience, it unfolds its genius steadily, but it is probably best approached after you are well acquainted with the *B minor Mass*. Hearing recordings of highlights, or just the choruses, would make sense as an introduction to the music, even if the impact of the story is inevitably diminished.

Other music

As mentioned at the beginning of this section, there are many other famous Bach works, and a deeper exploration might include:

- The six *Cello Suites* for unaccompanied cello.

- The three *Violin Sonatas* and three *Partitas* (suites) for unaccompanied violin.

- The seven *Harpsichord Concertos*, plus concertos for two, three and four harpsichords.

- *The Musical Offering*, usually arranged for chamber orchestra.

- *The Art of Fugue*, a series of fugues for harpsichord or chamber orchestra.

- The *Goldberg Variations*, a set of 30 variations for harpsichord.

- *The Well-tempered Clavier*, 48 preludes and fugues for harpsichord.

- The *St. John Passion*, Bach's other setting of the Passion story.

- The *Christmas Oratorio*, a choral work for Christmas, comprising six cantatas.

58

And there are, of course, the cantatas themselves, of which the *Hunt Cantata*, the *Coffee Cantata*, the *Peasant Cantata*, and *Wachet Auf* are amongst the best known. As you can see, not all Bach's cantatas are religious ones!

Bach wrote some amazingly accessible works, and many more that give up their glories only with more effort. Be patient, and don't be put off if you come across a work that leaves you cold. Put it to one side, recognising that it is not for you yet.

6

SCHUBERT

Schubert *His Life*

Franz Peter Schubert was born on January 31, 1797. He was the 12th child of 14 (five surviving infancy) born to Franz Theodor Florian Schubert and his wife Elizabeth. His father was a schoolmaster who eventually owned his own school and lived in a suburb of Vienna.

Schubert grew up in a family with three elder brothers and a younger sister. The family was not badly off financially, and as was to be expected of a schoolteacher's son, Schubert had a good education, including music, which his father supervised. He grew up with a piano in the house.

Schubert developed into a competent practising musician on the piano, violin, and viola. He started composing at the age of five, songs being his favourite form, and he was a good singer himself. His singing teacher 'had never had such a pupil'. At the age of 12, Schubert was accepted into the choir of the Imperial Royal Seminary – a top choir in Vienna, as demonstrated by the fact that the Court Composer Salieri selected the membership. The young choirboy started on his musical career at a momentous time: Haydn was at the end of his life, Beethoven was in his prime, Napoleon was laying siege to Vienna and the city was wracked by serious food shortages.

Schubert played in the school orchestra, and was quickly recognized as an extremely talented musician in the making. He turned increasingly to composing, writing overtures, songs, and string quartets, and this led to him receiving lessons from Salieri.

Schubert stayed at the Seminary until 1812, when his voice broke. He turned down the offer of a further scholarship, and trained instead to become a schoolteacher, in order to earn money. In 1813, he completed his first symphony – an attractive piece occasionally played today

– and in 1814, when he was 17 years old, he conducted a Mass in the first public performance of his music. Salieri was amongst the audience.

On October 19 in the same year, Schubert's brilliance as a great composer of songs ('lieder' in German) shone out with his setting of *Gretchen at the Spinning Wheel* from 'Faust', by the great German poet, Goethe. Schubert's musical setting brought a new dimension to Goethe's work, and its success led him to write no fewer than 300 further songs over the next two years – a burst of creativity akin to Mozart's, but here finding its inspiration specifically in song writing.

1815 and 1816 saw Schubert's symphonic expertise develop, culminating in the beautiful *Fifth Symphony*, and by now music was becoming increasingly important compared with teaching. He contributed to the celebration of Salieri's 50th anniversary in Vienna, received his first commission (for a cantata), and finally made the decision to give up general teaching as a career. For the rest of his life he was a full-time composer.

The next year Schubert met a man who was to become his spokesman in the world of music, an opera singer named Johann Michael Vogl. An extremely tall man, with an outstanding baritone voice, Vogl was highly intelligent with an imposing personality. The two were to become one of the great musical partnerships: the composer and his singer, as sublime in performance as comic in contrast (the young and the old – Vogl was nearly fifty – the short and the tall, the plump and the slim).

Their progress was interrupted however by Schubert's need to find new lodgings, and after a brief spell back at his father's school, he took up a post as music teacher to an aristocrat's two daughters, 100 miles from Vienna. This pleasant country interlude lasted until November 1818, when he returned to Vienna to share a room with an artist friend. 1819 saw the fulfilment of a commission for a quintet based on his song *Die Forelle* (The Trout), and so was born one of his most gloriously happy works.

Schubert had a group of close friends, a rather Bohemian crowd, artistic, but not so talented as himself. They were somewhat radical and outspoken, and one of them was even deported for insulting behaviour to the State, censorship being strong at that time. Schubert was involved in this incident, and achieved a police record as a result. The friends would typically gather in one of Vienna's coffee-houses and set the world to rights, sometimes breaking into impromptu concerts, and carrying on into the early hours of the morning. This group started to break up in 1820, and for whatever reason, this was not a great year for Schubert's compositions. An opera commission, *The Magic Harp*, was unsuccessful, as was another opera attempt. Schubert was never to achieve any recognition as an operatic composer.

In 1821, Schubert went to live with the family of his friend Schober. Conditions there were extremely comfortable, and his fortunes started to improve. The social life was good, including 'Schubertiads' – the name given by participants to their entertaining evenings involving music and wine, the music supplied by Schubert. These two years until 1823 were to be his happiest. The *Unfinished Symphony* was his major work of this period – a work of extreme sensitivity, which saw the maturity of his symphonic technique, but which he never completed.

Schubert never got close to marriage. Small, shy, unattractive and lacking confidence with women, he had consorted instead with prostitutes or 'women of easy virtue'. As a result, he contracted syphillis, at that time a fatal disease. Slow-acting, but inevitable, it was to eat away at his health throughout the 1820s, but with substantial periods of remission. He spent some of 1823 in hospital, and sought the best medical advice.

Schubert attended the great musical event of Vienna in 1824 – the premiere of Beethoven's *Ninth Symphony*. Schubert was known to the reclusive, deaf Beethoven, but they had not met. Schubert's main reputation was as a song writer, and his failure as an opera composer led him to concentrate instead on chamber and instrumental music when not writing for the voice. Thus, the last years saw his greatest piano compositions and string quartets – the latter performed by the same top Viennese quartet which gave the first performances of the celebrated late masterpieces by Beethoven.

The rest of 1824 and 1825 were taken up with composing and travel, visiting friends (with many impromptu concerts) outside Vienna, frequently in the company of his friend and interpreter, Vogl. It is now thought that Schubert wrote his magnificent *Ninth Symphony* – long thought to have been composed in 1828 – during September 1825.

At last a reasonable number of Schubert's songs were being published, although publishers, as usual, wanted simple, popular music, and were little interested in difficult-to-play works of genius. 1826 was a year of recurring illness and recovery, but included the composition of his last string quartet.

During Beethoven's last illness, in March 1827, the two great composers finally met. It is remarkable that they did not develop a relationship (although several stories suggest that they met earlier), but perhaps it was due to Schubert's shyness combined with the young man's awe of the aging Beethoven. On March 27, Beethoven died, and Schubert was one of the torchbearers at the funeral two days later.

Later that year he spent an idyllic month in Graz amongst music-loving friends. It was a period of great happiness for Schubert, and inspiration flowed unabated. March 26, 1828, saw the first, and only, all-Schubert concert. It was a sell-out, and described by one listener as 'glorious', but it received little publicity, due to the eruption on Vienna three days later of the demonic violin virtuoso, Paganini.

This Schubert concert was the artistic peak of his career. While preparing for it, he revised his *Ninth Symphony* for a planned performance by the Vienna Philharmonic Society, but they viewed it as too long and difficult to be played. The manuscript then vanished, and the symphony was miraculously rediscovered by the composer Robert Schumann 10 years later.

Schubert composed his extraordinary *String Quintet* and the last three piano sonatas in the same year, but in the autumn his health caved in. He took to his bed on November 11, and died at 3p.m. on the 19th, in his brother Ferdinand's house in a suburb of Vienna. He was buried two days later by his family and friends, with his last wish, to lie close to Beethoven, being fulfilled.

His passing had none of the state-funeral impact of Beethoven's death. He died the youngest of the acknowledged great composers, having accomplished more than anyone other than Mozart in his 31 years. He was still relatively unknown, and it was many years before even some of his greatest works were published. Some were lucky not to be lost for ever. The poet Grillparzer's epitaph for Schubert's tombstone reads:

The Art of Music here entombed a rich possession
But even far fairer hopes.

Schubert *The Person*

Franz Schubert was short, probably less than five foot tall, and of stocky build. As a youth he had a mop of curly brown hair over his round face, but was balding a little in his twenties. Being short-sighted, he always wore a distinctive pair of small, round-lensed glasses, which he even wore on top of his head in bed. A friend described him as looking like a 'drunken cabby'!

He was a gregarious and natural person with the many friends with whom he socialised constantly. Outside his circle he was shy. He was inherently good-natured, lived a Bohemian life and was never well enough known for fame to alter his preferred lifestyle. He was not interested in being smartly dressed. He inspired a lot of affection from his friends and was a leading light amongst his artistic circle. Schubert himself was not a forceful personality, but was very influential within the group.

Intelligent, from a well-educated family, Schubert was well-read, and a discerning judge of material for his songs. He was independently minded and radical in his political views. He was particularly shy with women, and kept his deepest emotions to himself. He apparently did not even have sufficient self-confidence to arrange to meet his idol Beethoven. With friends he was open and honest rather than politic, with a fierce temper when aroused, for example by ill-informed views on music. Social and fun-loving, he happily over-indulged with wine at the late night parties he loved so much.

Schubert was a romantic, and his strong emotions provided fertile drive for his prodigious musical talent. He was highly industrious, and felt his purpose in the world was to compose.

Schubert *The Music*

Schubert had a marvellous melodic gift, and is therefore a composer of widespread appeal. It is difficult not to be attracted by his music, abounding with good tunes, and usually evoking a very positive mood. Schubert usually leaves you feeling better for having listened to him.

For the 'Schubert Starterpack' I suggest you try the following examples of his works:

1 Symphonies The *Unfinished Symphony* captures the best of Schubert. The quiet opening creates a mood of supreme confidence and calm in which Schubert's lovely melodies cast their spell. Sonorous orchestral climaxes alternate with pastoral peace. The second and last movement is slower, and opens with a yearning theme for the violins. Sadness is never far away in this hypnotic music, as in a haunting theme introduced first by the clarinet. The rapt mood is punctuated by a powerful march rhythm where the woodwind play their melody valiantly against the rest of the orchestra, but the exquisite calm always returns. The symphony seems perfect without the missing movements that Schubert never got round to writing.

2 Chamber music The *Trout Quintet* (the German title, 'Die Forelle', sounds so much more attractive) is a catchy and happy work, with Schubert's musical invention in full flow. There is not a dull moment in any of the five movements. Full chords on the strings are answered by the piano to set the work in motion, and a lively allegro ensues, melting regularly into delicate touches. Schubert's piano writing, as always, is a delight. The high spot of the quintet is the set of variations on the theme of the song which gives the quintet its name. It is introduced gently and sweetly, and then Schubert gives it the full treatment – ornate, jaunty, aggressive, intimate, and joyful in turn. The ensuing finale spins along like a wild peasant's dance, to provide a great conclusion.

3 Piano music Schubert's distinctive piano sound is heard to marvellous effect in his *Impromptus*, eight short pieces for solo piano, in two groups, Opus 90 and Opus 142. They are amongst the most appealing works in the whole of the piano repertoire, simple melodies that can melt and bring peace to your heart. Schubert had the knack of writing lovely accompaniments to his main themes, and the *First Impromptu* of Opus 90 is as good an example as any. It develops considerable passion, and the emotional range is very wide. The *Third Impromptu*, with its hymn-like theme over rippling accompaniment is a personal favourite of mine: it creates a remarkable sense of restfulness, an ideal stress-reducer.

4 Songs To select a first sample of Schubert's songs is no easy matter, since there are the hundreds of individual settings of poems, and also the song cycles – related sets of poems. Settling for the favourites is probably the best path, and a recital disc could well include the touching *An die Musik*; the original version of *Die Forelle*; the demonic *Erlkönig* where the father, riding with his infant son through the night, loses him to the devil; the love-sick *Gretchen am Spinnrade* with its hypnotic and descriptive piano accompaniment; the famous setting of the *Ave Maria*; the enchanting *An Sylvia*; and the radiant *Ganymed*. Schubert's interpretation of the texts is second to none, as the voice and piano accompaniment convey the rich meanings of the poetry. It is important to follow the translations of words initially for a full appreciation.

In the works above you will find the essence of Schubert. Set out here are the next steps in exploring his music.

Symphonies

Apart from the *Unfinished*, Schubert wrote just one other major symphonic masterpiece, his *Ninth Symphony*. It opens with a pensive horn call and a very pregnant introduction, which gradually winds itself up and launches into a spiky allegro. A more relaxed theme follows, into which intrude some stately trombones. Terrific momentum is soon built up and maintained to the noble conclusion of the movement. The following andante is march-like, a perky theme which Schubert develops in many guises. The scherzo is fast-moving and has a ravishing middle section of mournful singing woodwind. The last movement is an orchestral tour-de-force, in which fanfares set off an extraordinary scampering theme on the violins. This finale has great vitality, and it's difficult to prevent yourself swaying to its persistent rhythms. The movement builds to a climax where fanfares and rhythms unite in joyful celebration.

The symphonies of Schubert's youth are much lighter works, but they have a unique charm and lyricism and are a delight to listen to. The first three, in particular, deserve greater popularity.

The *Fifth Symphony* has a magical first movement, from its first bars, when the woodwind ushers in a theme of elegant simplicity on the strings. The slow movement flows along steadily, sometimes serene, sometimes ardent, before dying away with a falling horn call. A sturdy minuet precedes a finale of considerable panache.

The stately introduction of the *Third Symphony* launches into an allegro with a remarkable warbling clarinet theme of instant appeal. The allegretto second movement has a middle section of melting delight, and is followed by a rumbustuous minuet. The finale is fleet-footed and exhilarating, full of fun and momentum. Not to be missed!

In terms of structure, the *First* and *Second Symphonies* are a matched pair. Slow introductions leading into lively and catchy first movements are followed by singing andantes, minuets that are in the manner of Mozart and Haydn respectively, and playful finales that absolutely fizz along.

The *Fourth* and *Sixth Symphonies* remain for further exploration, attractive works in which Schubert's style was in transition. The Seventh probably never existed.

Chamber music

There are many treasures in these intimate works, none finer than Schubert's *String Quintet*, one of the greatest compositions in the total chamber music repertoire. A slow introduction leads into a dramatic first theme which gives way to a gorgeous, gentle melody. The adagio is no less than sublime, with one violin and cello quietly unfolding a heart-breaking theme. The mood is broken by an agitated outburst, only for the opening theme to return with greater intensity. In the middle of a fiery scherzo lies a section of extraordinary quality, of which Anthony Mann wrote 'Down and down the music sinks as it hesitates before entering a dark abyss of almost unbearable isolation'. The finale allows a degree of relief, but not so much as to diminish the impact of the totality.

The *Octet* adds clarinet, horn, bassoon and double bass to the normal string quartet to create a rich sound palette and a unique work. Its six movements give wide variety of mood, but from the opening chords of the adagio introduction it is clear that we are listening to a substantial masterpiece. The movements are: *allegro, adagio, scherzo, variations, minuet, and allegro*. The clarinet imbues the work with a nostalgic mood in the first two movements. The jaunty scherzo is followed by a rich set of variations with different instruments taking prominence in turn. Nostalgia returns for the minuet. At the opening of the finale, tremolando strings set a mood of drama which is dispersed by the happy and lyrical themes that follow. In a stroke of genius Schubert brings back the dramatic opening before launching the exhilarating final bars.

The *String Quartet No.14*, known by the title *Death and the Maiden* from the song of that title which provides the theme for the slow movement, opens with dramatic chords out of which emerge a restless and busy allegro. The music moves on into one of Schubert's heart-melting second themes. The variations movement opens in hushed reverence, and the theme undergoes several energetic transformations before finally returning to a mood of peace. After the minuet, a galloping presto completes the quartet.

The *Piano Trio No.1*, like Beethoven's *Archduke*, opens with a supremely confident theme, setting the mood for one of Schubert's masterpieces. The second theme is lyrical in contrast. First the cello and then the violin introduces the extended and graceful slow movement melody, creating a rapt and tranquil mood, ideal night-time listening. After the scherzo, Schubert provides a gloriously inventive and jaunty finale. His treatment of the second theme – which Bruckner would have loved as a scherzo – leads ultimately to a magical and bouncy passage where the three instruments take it in gentle turns to play the spikey theme against an accompaniment like pealing bells.

The *String Quartet No.13* opens with a yearning theme over a pulsating accompaniment. The slow movement has an immediately appealing theme for Schubert to exploit. The minuet, with its call to arms from the cello, is one of his most attractive, slow and lyrical, touching both light and serious moods. The finale is highly rhythmic. Schubert wrote one further mature string quartet, *No.15*, and the earlier works are attractive. His other chamber music includes the outstanding *Piano Trio No.2*.

Piano music

Schubert's piano music is rich territory. His piano style is as distinctive as that of Mozart, Beethoven or Chopin, and his invention no less. If you are taken with the *Impromptus*, or the piano accompaniment to the songs, you will gain much pleasure exploring his piano repertoire. There are 21 piano sonatas in the catalogue, of which the last eight are masterpieces from his maturity, and there are miscellaneous other works.

Piano Sonata No.18, which the composer Robert Schumann considered to be 'the most perfect in form and spirit', opens with gentle peals of chords enunciating the most simple basis for a theme: a couple of notes that Schubert develops into a formidable movement, and which enchant each time they return. The andante provides wide contrasts of reflective beauty and powerful statements. There are marvellous examples of Schubert's lingering endings, a skill where he had no rival. The minuet is a delight, with a ravishing middle section, and the finale provides a lighthearted end.

Schubert's *Piano Sonata No.21*, his last, is a magnificent work from its opening bars, when he introduces his simple and lovely theme with a great sense of inexorable forward momentum. Schubert takes over 20 minutes in this exploration. The slow movement is intense, a melancholic theme gradually emerging out of the background. Schubert brings solace as only he can in the middle section. 'Con delicatezza' (with delicacy) is the very apt marking for the magical scherzo, and the finale has a fine melody which Schubert treats in serious vein.

Piano Sonata No.16 opens with an arresting rhythmic motto which dominates the first movement. The andante starts in Schubert's inimitable lyrical style, but his creativity then takes off with energy in different directions before coming gently to rest. The scherzo is fast and percussive except for the lullaby-like middle section, the finale has an urgent accompaniment and numerous short phrases that quickly impress on the memory.

The *Wanderer Fantasia* is Schubert's most virtuoso piano composition, comprising just one movement. The opening highly rhythmic theme pervades the work, but there is enormous variety of mood between the four sections, and in particular in the second, a set of variations on a theme from Schubert's song *Der Wanderer*. The Fantasia combines beauty and brilliance.

Schubert's song cycles

It is unrealistic to attempt to chart an ideal path through Schubert's hundreds of songs, but if you like the most famous ones there is little risk in trying more. However, Schubert wrote several song-cycles, linked sets of songs, which make for very rewarding listening experiences.

In *Die Winterreise* (Winter's Journey) Schubert set to music all the 24 poems in Wilhelm Müller's text. The melancholic tale of the lonely traveller moved Schubert deeply, and he created a marvellous portrayal of mood and a bleak winter landscape. It starts with *Gute Nacht* (Goodnight) with its trudging piano accompaniment, as the traveller unhappily leaves an unrequited love and starts his journey. Titles such as *The Weathercock, Frozen Tears, Numbness*, indicate the content of this masterpiece. If you project yourself into the troubadour's position, the work is graphic. The most appealing song is perhaps *Der Lindenbaum* (the Lime Tree), but the strength of the cycle is the sense of continuity in spite of varied episodes, a true journey.

Die Schöne Müllerin (The Beautiful Maid of the Mill) consists of settings of 20 poems, also by Müller, of the unrequited love of another wanderer who finds a water-mill and falls for the young girl who lives there. The stream plays an important part throughout, leading the troubadour to the mill initially, providing the final refuge of despair at the very end. The songs have great variety of mood as they tell the sad tale. From the opening *Wandering* with its happy mood and typically jaunty piano accompaniment, through the plaintive *Morning Greeting*, to the final lament *The Stream's Lullaby*, Schubert again creates a marvellously varied yet integrated work.

Schwanengesang (Swan Song) is a grouping of 14 songs composed from two sets of poems, together with the last song Schubert wrote. It opens with a song called *Love's Message* where the poet asks the rushing brook to take a message to his loved one. Schubert's piano accompaniment brilliantly conjures up the image of the stream. This is typical of the first seven songs set to texts by the poet Ludwig Rellstab, beautiful, evocative, and not too serious in mood. The last, entitled *Farewell*, is a philosophical parting, gratitude for good times. The six settings of Heinrich Heine's poems that follow are largely concerned with stress and despair. In the first one, *Atlas*, the poet has the weight of the world on his shoulders: in the last, *The Doppelganger*, Schubert creates an appropriate ghostly setting. *Pigeon Post* is a lovely and light-hearted, if inappropriate, finale.

Hector Berlioz

7

BERLIOZ

Berlioz *His Life*

*L*ouis-Hector Berlioz was born on December 11, 1803, in the small village of La Côte-St.-André, 30 miles from Grenoble in France. His father, Louis-Joseph, was an excellent physician and quite well off; his mother, Marie-Antoinette-Josephine, came from a well respected family.

Hector Berlioz (as he was called) was the oldest of six children, but one of his sisters died at the age of eight, and a brother at three. The family was well educated, closely knit, lived in a healthy rural community and took a lively interest in music. Berlioz took up the flute. A highly intelligent boy, he began writing modest compositions by the age of 12.

His very romantic traits were revealed early when, at the age of 11, he had a crush on an attractive 18-year-old called Estelle. His interest in music was encouraged through composition lessons with the village music teacher, and he was heavily involved in chamber music concerts in the village, both playing and composing. A new music master took his accomplishments further with composition and guitar lessons.

In 1821, he left for Paris with one of his cousins to study medicine, but early experience of the dissecting rooms and the morgue put him off a career as a doctor. In Paris he soon discovered the opera, and in particular Gluck's *Iphigénie en Tauride*. His medical studies only lasted a year before the College of Medicine closed for six months due to political unrest, and this gave him time to study music. He could be found regularly in the library of the Conservatoire, pouring over operatic scores, copying them, and learning them, and it was at this time that he first arranged for the publication of some of his songs.

Berlioz managed to get himself accepted as a pupil of a well-known teacher and composer, the elderly Le Sueur. Their relationship became a close one, and very helpful to Berlioz' development. Berlioz soon decided that he was going to be a composer – an unsavoury prospect for his respectable and conservative family, and rows about his musical career were rife at home for several years.

1824 saw him back in Paris, composing a Mass (later destroyed), which was performed for the first time on July 10, 1825, with considerable success. Much encouraged, Berlioz entered for the annual Prix de Rome, the major national award for composition to a prescribed text, but it was 1831 before he was to win this prize, with its considerable grant and travel opportunities. As a result of the failure of his first attempt, Berlioz enrolled at the Conservatoire. His second attempt, a cantata entitled *Mort d'Orphée* (Death of Orpheus) was too revolutionary to get the prize it deserved. The musical establishment and Berlioz were not yet compatible.

In 1827, Berlioz discovered Shakespeare when he attended a performance of '*Hamlet*' by an English touring company in Paris. Harriet Smithson was the actress playing Ophelia, and Berlioz fell into romantic love. On Harriet's part, Berlioz was just another fan, but he was thrown into deep emotional turmoil. Early the next year, Berlioz heard Beethoven's *Third* and *Fifth Symphonies* for the first time, and these had as great an impact as Shakespeare had done. In the summer, he read Goethe's play, '*Faust*', expanding even further his dramatic and artistic horizons.

This was a time of enormous creative experience for Berlioz. He composed his Opus 1, *Eight Scenes from Faust*, and then his obsession with Harriet Smithson and the experience of Beethoven's symphonic genius resulted in the remarkable *Symphonie Fantastique* in 1830. The titles of the five movements indicate the highly programmatic and autobiographical elements in the work: *Dreams-passions*; *A Ball*; *Scene in the Fields*; *March to the Scaffold* and *Witches' Sabbath*.

Sanity was restored when he succumbed to the charms of a highly attractive 18-year-old pianist called Camille Moke, who – unlike Harriet – returned his affections. They planned to marry, but Berlioz won the Prix de Rome that year, and after the successful premiere of his new symphony, he went off to Italy. His surging progress and recognition in Paris came to a halt, and Camille's mother had the opportunity to develop a more secure future for her daughter.

Life in Rome was relaxed. Berlioz mixed with other artists (including the composer Mendelssohn), and walked frequently in the surrounding countryside, but in compositional terms, it was a fallow period. Drama erupted suddenly when Camille's mother wrote to tell him that her daughter was to marry a piano manufacturer. Berlioz set off for Paris, disguised as a lady's maid, complete with pistols to kill Camille, her prospective husband, and himself. However, by the time he had travelled as far as Nice he had calmed down, so he composed two overtures there and returned to Rome. *Lélio*, a sequel to the *Symphonie Fantastique*, was the main work composed during the remaining time in Rome.

Berlioz returned to Paris in November 1832, refreshed and creatively ready to establish himself as France's leading composer. His life became a hectic routine of conducting performances of his works, and creating new ones.

Harriet Smithson was present at the first combined performance of the *Symphonie Fantastique* and *Lélio*, and soon afterwards, Berlioz and Harriet were formally introduced. His old obsession was re-activated, this time with success and they married in October 1833, with Liszt, the famous pianist who had become an intimate friend of Berlioz, as witness. A son, Louis, was born the next year.

The greatest violin virtuoso of the 19th century, the demonic Paganini, also attended a performance of the *Fantastique* and was so taken with Berlioz' genius that he commissioned a viola concerto from him. So was born *Harold in Italy*, but Berlioz chose to compose a symphony with a prominent viola part, whereas Paganini had been looking for a virtuoso concerto to show off his skills, and lost interest.

To succeed as a composer in Paris, it was necessary to have success at the Opéra. Berlioz finally found a satisfactory libretto, and the years between 1834 and 1838 were taken up with the creation of *Benvenuto Cellini*. Immediately afterwards, he received a commission for a Requiem Mass from the Ministry of Arts. The opportunity for a large scale work appealed enormously to Berlioz, and he wrote this mighty music in the summer of 1837. He was later to say 'If only one of my works should survive, I plead mercy for my *Requiem*.'

The first performance was cancelled, and it required considerable pressure before the work could be launched in the church of Les Invalides in Paris on December 5, to celebrate the life of a French general.

If the *Requiem* was a stunning success, *Benvenuto Cellini* was not. It was not welcomed by the Opéra – too original, too different, and by Berlioz – and its first performance, in September 1838, was a disaster. Berlioz withdrew it six months later, and in many ways – in spite of it being a marvellous composition – it did irreparable damage to his chances of being recognized as France's musical genius.

Paganini heard *Harold in Italy* – the work he had rejected – at the end of this year. In one of the most generous gestures in the history of music, the violinist gave Berlioz a gift of 20,000 francs, an enormous sum for Berlioz, which enabled him to put his affairs in order. It also allowed him to reduce his activities as a music critic, a financially necessary job at which he was outstanding, but which made him quite a few enemies.

He immediately set to writing a new symphony, using Shakespeare's 'Romeo and Juliet' as its theme. This was first performed on November 26, 1839. A second government commission, to celebrate the tenth anniversary of the 1830 revolution, resulted in the *Grande Symphonie Funèbre et Triomphale*, a ceremonial work in which Berlioz led massed military bandsmen through Paris in its first performance in July 1840.

The 1840s were to mark a change in Berlioz' career. His productivity diminished, and he increasingly escaped the Parisian apathy to his music in order to perform his now numerous compositions abroad. His marriage no longer interested him, and he took his new mistress, Marie Recio, with him on tours to Brussels and Germany in 1842/3. He visited Mendelssohn, Wagner, and Schumann, and was received by royalty; his music was acclaimed.

Return to Paris resulted only in him writing about music, not composing. Harriet, her acting career long over, was drinking increasingly heavily (being married to Berlioz could not have been easy), but 1845 saw him off to Vienna and Prague where he received the greatest acclaim of his career. On this tour, which lasted seven months, inspiration returned at last and he composed *The Damnation of Faust*. This concert opera (for performance in the concert hall rather than the theatre), though a brilliant work, was greeted with apathy at its premiere in Paris, so who can blame Berlioz for setting off again, this time to Russia.

Abroad it was nothing but acclaim. The Russian concerts were magnificent, and on his way back he performed *Faust* in Berlin with great success, and with the support of the King of Prussia. Next, he was off to London for eight months, while France was again in a state of revolution. It was at this time that he started to write his memoirs, one of the great artistic autobiographies.

Another great composition followed. The *Te Deum* appeared in the year after his return to Paris, but as was becoming typical, it didn't achieve its first performance until much later, in 1855.

Berlioz was back in London in 1851 and again in 1852, as an orchestral conductor, increasingly performing other composers' works as well as his own. But although the 1851 visit to London prevented him from attending his friend Liszt's staging of *Benvenuto Cellini* at Weimar, he was able to attend the Berlioz Festival there in November 1852.

Harriet died in 1854, and shortly after, Berlioz married Marie Recio, a practical rather than a romantic decision. Meanwhile, his son Louis, who had caused him much anguish, was embarked on a naval career. In London, Berlioz spent time with Wagner, who was on a similar conducting mission. Later, in Weimar, whilst staying with Franz Liszt, Berlioz allowed himself to be persuaded by Liszt's mistress, the Princess Sayn-Wittgenstein, to realise his ultimate operatic ambition: *The Trojans* – a mammoth task which he completed in 1858, having written the libretto as well as the music.

The Trojans only received its first full performance in 1951, in London, although after much politicking and negotiation it was staged in part in Paris, in 1863. Berlioz' health had by now started to decline, the illness showing itself particularly as a severe intestinal pain, but still he persevered, writing, travelling, conducting, and at times composing. His last work was the comic opera *Beatrice and Benedict*, based on Shakespeare's play '*Much Ado About Nothing*', and it was completed and performed successfully in 1862.

Berlioz' last years were those of a sad, sick, embittered, and neglected genius. His second wife died in 1862. There were highlights however: searching out, in adolescent fantasy, the first love of his life, Estelle, now a widow; a final, acclaimed, visit to Vienna to conduct *The Damnation of Faust* in 1866; and a similar trip to Russia the next year. Between these two musical trips, he was shattered by the news of the death of his son Louis from yellow fever in the West Indies.

In 1868, on holiday in the South of France, Berlioz suffered two strokes. He withdrew into a reclusive life back in Paris, needing his servant to feed him. He saw only close friends, and some were by his bedside when he passed away on March 8, 1869. His funeral was impressive, a band accompanying the cortege, and an orchestra in the church. The music included excerpts from his *Requiem* and that of Mozart. The composers Gounod and Bizet were amongst many mourners from France's artistic elite.

Berlioz *The Person*

Hector Berlioz was slight of build, with very distinctive features. His friend, the composer Ferdinand Hiller, described him thus: 'the high forehead, precipitously overhanging the great, curving hawk nose; the thin finely-cut lips; the rather short chin; the enormous shock of light brown hair against the fantastic wealth of which the barber could do nothing.'

He had great energy, initiative, and self-belief, and was often outspoken and arrogant. He had, initially, the brash confidence of youth, and would always speak up for what he believed in. He thought little of the consequences of his actions, preferring to let the world have his opinions. He could arouse hostility in people who stood in his path. He couldn't stand incompetence or hypocrisy, and he had a sharp tongue and caustic wit.

He was highly intelligent, and largely self-taught in music. His talents also extended to writing, in which he had a successful career. He did not write only on musical subjects, and his memoirs make one of the most fascinating autobiographies by an artist. One senses that he could have been successful in any chosen field.

He was an idealist, a great romantic, and a revolutionary, and, until his later years, many of his actions reflected this. Perhaps the failure of his marriage to Harriet Smithson brought him back to a more realistic approach to life, but to matters he believed in, he brought a consuming passion. In the main, his life seldom seemed truly happy, but was usually exciting.

Berlioz *The Music*

Berlioz could write works of the greatest delicacy, or of overwhelming simple power. He had a vivid imagination, and great originality, particularly in the early years of his career.

It is almost impossible today to realise how revolutionary his most famous work, the *Symphonie Fantastique*, must have sounded in 1830. It is a work that holds the interest throughout its five contrasting movements, and it culminates in a terrifying march to the guillotine (you hear the head drop into the basket), and the macabre *Witches' Sabbath*. Truly fantastic, you can enter Berlioz' dreams and nightmares, and experience his unique handling of an orchestra.

No Berlioz work is more exquisitely crafted than his song-cycle *Nuits d'Été* (Nights of Summer). A loose set of six songs, written for a variety of voices, but usually sung by a mezzo-soprano and orchestra, it makes a ravishing experience with its highly evocative mood-setting. The love songs *Spectre of the Rose* and *Absence* are particularly seductive.

Another great contrast is the mighty *Te Deum*, a six movement setting for large orchestra, chorus, and organ. From the imperious opening chords on the organ, with orchestral accompaniment, to the obsessive hammered rhythm of the last movement – when it climaxes as only a Berlioz work can, with ceremonial trumpets, organ and orchestra – it is in turn beautiful and tremendously exciting. The magnificence of this work still seeks wider recognition, and it is enthralling in live performance.

For some purely orchestral music, there are the overtures, relatively short and brilliant, full of Berlioz' originality, and great fun to listen to. *Roman Carnival* has always been a showcase for a virtuoso orchestra, and the others, including *King Lear*, *Waverley*, and *Les Francs Juges*, all have their own Berliozian character.

Berlioz' *Dramatic Symphony, Romeo and Juliet*, contains some of his most acclaimed music, comprising some purely orchestral movements, others accompanied by solo voice or chorus – all necessary to portray the great unfolding romantic tragedy. At the heart of this work is the *Scene of Love*, as passionate and beautiful a movement as you could wish for. The full seven movement work lasts about 80 minutes, and many performances economise by selecting just the purely orchestral movements.

Harold in Italy is a symphony with a prominent viola part which depicts the subject, Harold (created by the poet Byron), in four different situations – *Harold in the mountains*; *March of the Pilgrims*; *Serenade of a Mountaineer of the Abruzzi to his mistress*, and *Orgy of the Brigands*. These scenes are based on Berlioz' own experiences in Italy. The work is full of melody, though less brightly textured than the *Symphonie Fantastique* due to the prominence of the viola part and a reduced dynamic scale. It is both reflective and evocative.

The most overwhelming and magnificent of Berlioz' compositions is the *Requiem – Le Grand Messe des Morts*. Lasting about an hour and a half, its nine sections maintain a highly dramatic tension and contrast throughout. The build-up to the Day of Judgement, and its depiction, is one of the great experiences in all music, particularly if heard live in a suitable spacious acoustic such as a cathedral, or London's Royal Albert Hall. The eruption of the four brass bands in the four corners of a cathedral, each chanting its separate part, is nothing short of sensational, and the Requiem is a work that I would travel many miles to hear.

The concert opera *The Damnation of Faust* is also a truly exciting work, depicting the tale of Faust, who sells his soul to the devil, Mephistopheles, and loses his love, Marguerite. The story is ideally suited to Berlioz' dramatic and romantic instincts, which are magnificently realised, and the music has that searing power of greatness. The passionate opening scene is followed by a full-blooded peasants' chorus and the famous and exhilarating *Hungarian March*. Many further delights include the rival choruses for the soldiers and students, Mephistopheles' *Song of the flea*, and Margeurite's romantic *The burning flame of love*, with its melancholic cor anglais accompaniment, but everything builds to the inevitable climax. The last scenes are thrilling, containing some of Berlioz' most vivid music, as Faust cries despairingly to nature before embarking with Mephistopheles on the *Ride to the Abyss* and into Hell.

The work ends with a heavenly chorus of redemption and Marguerite's salvation.

Berlioz' epic operatic masterpiece, *The Trojans*, is a long work and best approached in highlights until the urge grabs you to undertake its full four hour length. It is the story of the fall of the city of Troy, the love of Aeneas – a Trojan hero – and Dido, the Queen of Carthage, and Aeneas' departure to build another city. The work is consistently inspired, and profoundly moving, particularly at the end, when Dido commits suicide and there is a vision of Rome. The arias have exceptional quality from the opening *The Greeks have vanished* to the last *Farewell, proud city*, and the famous *Trojan March* music – as the wooden horse containing the hidden Greeks is brought into the city – is enthralling.

Benvenuto Cellini is a fast moving comic opera, full of really good tunes, comedy and drama, and of normal operatic length. The story concerns the escapades of the Florentine goldsmith and sculptor, Cellini, his love for Teresa, and his problems in fulfilling a commission for the Pope. Berlioz has plenty of opportunity to display his touch with passionate music, humorous songs and thrilling choruses. The opera deserves to be much better known, but the same also applies to *The Trojans* and *The Damnation of Faust*. Berlioz is still the outstanding candidate amongst undervalued operatic composers.

Amongst Berlioz' other works should be mentioned:

- The *Symphonie Funèbre et Triomphale*, a three movement work largely written for military band, but with chorus and orchestra in the last movement, and very much a ceremonial work. Stirring!

- *The Childhood of Christ*, a Christmas oratorio of delicacy and originality.

Few works then, to represent Berlioz' life work, although there are others not considered appropriate here. They are highly original compositions which show his mastery of the orchestra, and a rich spirit.

8

VERDI

Verdi *His Life*

Giuseppe Verdi was born on October 9, 1813, in the small village of Le Roncole in the province of Parma, in Italy. The family had come down in the world and his father, Carlo, ran the inn and local store. Carlo had married an innkeeper's daughter, Luigia, in 1805, and Giuseppe was their first child. A daughter, Giuseppa, was born in 1816.

The local organist and music teacher discovered Giuseppe's musical talent, and persuaded Carlo to buy the boy a small, harpsichord-like instrument called a spinet. When his teacher died, the young Verdi took over as organist in the church. At the age of ten, he was sent to school in Busseto, a town three miles away, and took lodgings there. The school was excellent: Verdi's talent was recognised and he received a good education.

He avoided being channelled into the priesthood, and won sponsorship from a rich local merchant called Antonio Barezzi. Still the organist at Roncole, Verdi joined their very musical household in Busseto. Barezzi had founded the local Philharmonic Society, a small group of the town's musicians. Verdi started composing and there was plenty of opportunity for his works to be performed by the band. He also fell in love with Barezzi's eldest daughter, Margherita.

In 1832, Verdi was turned down by the Milan Conservatory, a considerable blow to his pride. Barezzi paid for the only alternative, private tuition in Milan with Vincenzo Lavigna, an excellent teacher. Soon Verdi was given the opportunity to rehearse one of Milan's music societies, and he ended up giving the performance of Haydn's *Creation*, before the high society of the city.

Local politics held up his appointment in charge of music back in Busseto, but he finally made it in 1836 and married Margherita soon after. Although in a backwater again, after Milan, Verdi worked hard to keep his contacts there, and was soon negotiating to supply an opera. His wife gave birth to a daughter, Virginia, who died tragically in her second year, and to a son, Icilio.

In 1839 Verdi and his family set off for Milan, and his first opera, *Oberto*, was performed that autumn, but not before his son too had died. The opera was a considerable success, and Verdi received a commission for three more. Then a further disaster struck: his wife Margherita died. Verdi had to put his triple tragedy and the loss of his whole family to one side, and was forced back to composing.

His second opera was a flop, but soon afterwards he was – by lucky chance – given the libretto for *Nabucco*. It had its first performance in 1842, and it shot Verdi to instant fame. The chorus *Va pensiero* was to become the Italian song of freedom and achieve world fame. His next opera, *I Lombardi*, was another success soon after.

Verdi now met a young poet who was to become his librettist in many major successes – Francesco Maria Piave. They developed one of the great partnerships in operatic history, the first fruit of which was *Ernani*. It was clear that Verdi was becoming essentially a populist composer, appealing totally to the Italian people. The music critics of Europe were less impressed, but in Italy, he was a celebrity.

I due Foscari and *Joan of Arc* were the next operas to be completed as Verdi worked consistently hard on new projects, but he became seriously ill whilst composing *Attila* and had to take a very necessary break in the spring of 1846. After his recovery came *Macbeth* and a visit to London to conduct the premiere of *I Masnadieri* after which he went to Paris. Here he was joined by Giuseppina Strepponi, the woman he was to live with until her death fifty years later.

His mistress, Giuseppina, was an extremely talented singer, a couple of years younger than Verdi. She had experienced a difficult career, and produced three children whose paternity was complicated. However, she and the somewhat irascible Verdi, whom she had met some years earlier, were an extremely complementary match, and got on very well.

The Italian uprising in 1848 to expel the ruling Austrians was a patriotic cause close to Verdi's heart and he composed an opera with a similar theme, *The Battle of Legnano*, which was highly popular – until the Italians lost.

Verdi returned to live in Busseto in 1849, having acquired a large house and a farm. He was now quite well off, as he was an astute manager of money. However, the fact that he was living with his mistress, Giuseppina, caused a great scandal in the town, and Giuseppina was shunned.

Verdi continued to produce operas at regular intervals, *Luisa Miller* and *Stiffelio*, and Piave had by now completed a libretto called *Rigoletto* or *The Curse*. This text ran into trouble with the censors, as they considered it to be anti-royalty, so the characters were changed and *Rigoletto* had its premiere in Venice in 1851. It was a total success, and achieved fame throughout Europe.

As Verdi's name became increasingly well-known, so he became more reclusive. He moved to his farm-house in the country, Sant' Agata, where he was to live for the rest of his life, and became increasingly choosy about his friends and visitors.

His next operas were *Il Trovatore* (The Troubadour) and *La Traviata* (The Courtesan). The first was a great success, the latter a flop until he revised and relaunched it a year later, this time to great acclaim.

Verdi and Giuseppina left Italy in 1853 for a two year trip to France. There he was to create *The Sicilian Vespers* for the Paris Opéra. In spite of the usual trials of a new production in Paris, this opera too was a success.

When he returned to Italy, Verdi's life became split between managing the various estates where he invested his money, writing new compositions, engineering revivals, ensuring good conditions for performance, and trying to ensure that he was paid when his works were performed – copyright protection was very skimpy in Europe at this time. He met an outstanding conductor, Angelo Mariani, whose skills were to give Verdi further inspiration. Conducting, introducing greater control over an orchestra, was still a recent art.

Difficulty in finding dramatic librettos that were not too controversial was a consistent problem. In 1858 Verdi won a law suit brought against him by the opera house in Naples because he refused to go along with their demanded changes. Eventually *The Masked Ball* (based on the assassination of King Gustav the Third of Sweden) was given its first performance in Rome in 1859.

In the spring of 1859, war again broke out with the Austrians. The patriotic Verdi hoped for Italian independence, and played his part. His popularity and views led him to become a deputy in the Italian Parliament, although he was more a figurehead than an active politician. Verdi married Giuseppina later that year, but by then she was too old to have children, so they adopted a daughter, Maria.

It was two years before Verdi was able to take up composition again. *The Force of Destiny* was written for St. Petersburg in Russia and Verdi set off for its premiere in the autumn of 1862. He was travelling extensively at this time, and he did not complete his next opera, *Don Carlos*, which was written for Paris, until 1867.

1867 was not a good year. Verdi's father, Carlo, and his benefactor, Antonio Barezzi, both died, the latter's death particularly affecting Verdi. Also, Verdi's main librettist, Piave, suffered a stroke that was to leave him totally incapacitated until his death six years later.

Italy's great operatic composer Rossini died in November 1868 after many years of pleasurable retirement, and Verdi had the idea of celebrating the first anniversary of his death with a Requiem Mass, each movement of which was to be written by a different celebrity composer. Wrangling prevented its performance, and this composite work had to wait until recently for its premiere.

Verdi seems to have been in pretty tetchy mood at this time. He was foul to his conductor friend, Mariani; developed a passion for Mariani's fiancée, the soprano Teresa Stoltz – much to Giuseppina's dismay – and in general enhanced his reputation as a bit of an ogre.

A most unusual source for a commission appeared in 1870. The ruler of Egypt, a fan of Verdi, wanted a new work for the recently completed theatre in Cairo. August Mariette, a French member of his staff, wrote out a plot which was put to Verdi, who accepted it. Mariette had no experience of writing librettos, but his motivation was high, and *Aida* was born. After many delays, the opera had its premiere in Cairo in December 1871, all the sets having been prepared in Paris. It was a great success, but the composer was absent.

Verdi surprised his friends in the spring of 1873 with a performance of a string quartet he had composed during that winter, a vast change of style. The occasion for another very different type of work arose when the great Italian poet Manzoni, whom Verdi knew and greatly admired, died at the age of 87. Verdi composed a *Requiem* for the first anniversary of his death. This magnificent work was an immediate success, and Verdi was to perform it in many parts of Europe in the following year, including the newly built Albert Hall in London.

Verdi, now in his sixties, was a world celebrity. He was made a Senator in the Italian Parliament, and travelled much. His creative energies, not surprisingly, were burning less strongly. Revivals of his operas, and some revisions, took up most of his time.

Suddenly, in 1879, his interest was reawakened by the combination of Shakespeare's play 'Othello' and a quite exceptional librettist called Arrigo Boito. Boito, in addition to his writing skills, was also a well-known, if modestly successful, opera composer in his own right, and was therefore uniquely equipped to collaborate with Verdi.

Verdi had to be cajoled into writing the music, as he considered himself ready for retirement from composing operas. Discussions spread over several years before he actually started in 1884, and then he had a bust-up with Boito which created a further delay of a year. *Otello* finally had its premiere in February 1887, at La Scala, Milan, where so many of Verdi's operas had seen the light of day. The whole of the musical world was awaiting this late flowering from the greatest living operatic composer, and it was a great occasion in musical history.

One of the fruits of the success of *Otello* was that Verdi was able to finance two charities, a local hospital, and a home for elderly musicians in Milan. He composed an unaccompanied setting of the *Ave Maria* in 1889, and eventually, with the addition of three other choral pieces, including a *Te Deum*, the *Four Sacred Pieces* was completed in 1897.

Meanwhile, the wily Boito was dangling a sketch of a libretto based on Shakespeare's play, 'The Merry Wives of Windsor', in front of Verdi. Boito knew his man, and *Falstaff* was soon under way. The premiere took place at La Scala in February 1893, with – remarkably – Verdi conducting his new comedy masterpiece despite being in his 80th year. Three months later, a performance was given in Rome, with Verdi in the company of the King and Queen of Italy. The reception was overwhelming.

Boito tried his luck a third time with *King Lear*, another Shakespearian play that had tempted Verdi many times over the previous 50 years. But this time Verdi was too old, and they contented themselves with preparing the last two operas for Paris, where Verdi received the Grand Cross of the Légion d'Honneur from the French President.

Verdi's wife, Giuseppina, died in 1897. Verdi's last years were spent between Sant' Agata and Milan, where he had many friends. He had a heart attack and died on January 27, 1901. Thousands lined the streets for his funeral in Milan, and paid homage with the strains of his great national chorus *Va, pensiero*. Later, he was buried alongside his wife in the grounds of the rest home for musicians that he had founded.

Verdi *The Person*

Guiseppe Verdi was short, slightly built, with dark hair and a beard. He was a reticent person, and not easy to get on with. He was very shy in his early years and lacking in self-confidence. His success gradually overcame this handicap, and he became a famous and revered figure towards the end of his life, when he looked quite striking. He had strong emotions, but they were kept rigidly under control. He was a private person, and kept his domestic life from the public. He liked nothing better than to escape to his country estate.

Verdi was a man whose sympathies lay with ordinary people. He was independently-minded and strong in his opinions. He was quite prepared to ignore convention if he didn't agree with it. He was never a great socialiser, but over time he became more relaxed. He could be extremely courteous if he felt so inclined, he could also be quite brusque.

His business acumen was noteworthy, and he managed his affairs tightly. He drove a hard bargain over his operas, intent on ensuring that his family would never again be poor. He cared for the plight of old musicians and the sick, and invested his own money to help them, showing an altruistic side rare amongst great artists.

Verdi *His Operas*

Oberto (1839)

Un Giorno di Regno (1840)

Nabucco (1841)

I Lombardi (1843)

Ernani (1844)

I due Foscari (1844)

Giovanna d'Arco (1845)

Alzira (1845)

Attila (1846)

Macbeth (1847)

I Masnadieri (1847)

Jerusalem (1847)

Il Corsaro (1848)

La Battaglia di Legnano (1849)

Luisa Miller (1849)

Stiffelio (1850)

Rigoletto (1851)

Il Trovatore (1852)

La Traviata (1853)

Les Vêpres Siciliennes (1854)

Simon Boccanegra (1857)

Un Ballo in Maschera (1858)

La Forza del Destino (1862)

Don Carlos (1866)

Aida (1871)

Otello (1886)

Falstaff (1892)

Verdi *His Music*

As you can see from the listing of Verdi's operas, he was a prolific composer, particularly in his early years. His most popular works commence with *Rigoletto*, but increasingly today the early operas are becoming better known. Like the 27 piano concertos of Mozart, the 27 Verdi operas present a substantial feast for those who really fall for his attractive style.

To get the flavour and passion of Verdi, there is nothing better than to try the most popular pieces from the operas; ideally three selections, of tenor arias, of soprano arias, and of the great choruses.

Remember also that recordings of highlights are a good way to get to know each opera, and these are available for all the popular ones. Verdi was a shrewd and realistic operatic composer, however, and most of his operas last little more than two hours.

A good starting point is *Rigoletto*, an exciting tale with glorious music. The main characters are a rakish Duke, a hunchback court jester (Rigoletto) and his beautiful daughter, and the plot includes a curse and an assassination. There is never a dull moment, and the opera contains two of the most famous Verdi pieces, *La donna è mobile* and *Si, vendetta*. Keep a handkerchief for the end!

La traviata opens with an exquisite prelude of great emotion, appropriate for a tale of a sick courtesan, Violetta, who finds true love, but is forced to give it up. Verdi sets this tragedy to consistently lovely music, and as some of the scenes take place at a ball, there are a number of great, swirling, waltzes. The first of the three acts is particularly fine. The love music is extraordinarily moving, and the close of the opera is full of grief. Handkerchief again!

Otello follows the Shakespeare play closely, and shows the regression of the black Moor from a heroic and magnanimous leader to an insecure husband whose insane jealously leads him to murder his beautiful and loving white wife, Desdemona. The opera opens with an exciting storm scene as Otello's ship enters harbour. All the passion and intrigue is depicted in Verdi's music, and there are some great highspots – the opening chorus and Otello's marvellous entrance – the love duet between Otello and Desdemona when they are at last alone – the oath-taking between the evil Iago and Otello – Desdemona's *Willow Song* –

.and the final murder scene when Verdi brings back, with supreme poignancy, the theme from the first act when the lovers kissed. The ending is heartbreaking.

As a change from opera, this is a good time to introduce Verdi's *Requiem*, where his dramatic, operatic style links with the religious text to glorious effect. The work encompasses extremes, from the ethereal opening to a day of judgement where Verdi rivals Berlioz for earth-shattering music. Each of the seven movements is a masterpiece which rivets the attention, making the *Requiem* one of the great choral works.

The *Four Sacred Pieces* are not quite on the same plane. They do not form an integrated work like the *Requiem*, but are nonetheless lovely. The *Ave Maria* and *Laudi alla Vergine Maria* are for unaccompanied choirs; the *Stabat Mater* and *Te Deum* for full orchestra and chorus, and it is in these that Verdi is at his best. The *Te Deum*, which has many memorable themes, is outstanding. The cathedral musical tradition is very much present in these works, whereas the Requiem has its roots in the opera house.

Don Carlos may be one of Verdi's longest operas, but it is a searing experience. It is the story of the love of the King of Spain's son (Carlos) for his stepmother, and is rivetting from the opening sombre bars for trombones and horns, which create a great sense of expectancy. Verdi created an opera of enormous tension and passion, and endowed it with some of his greatest music. Already in the first act there are magnificent experiences – the glorious duet between Carlos and his friend Rodrigo, which Verdi caps with some of his most powerful music; the *Song of the Veil*, set after a lovely women's chorus; the love duet between Carlos and his queen; the shattering dialogue between King Phillip and Rodrigo. The ensuing music is no less fine, and has many highly dramatic scenes, including the auto-da-fè – the burning of the heretics, and the meeting between the King and the Grand Inquisitor. The last act, in a tomb, ends in sensational style, with Carlos dragged away by the ghost of his grandfather, Charles the Fifth.

Aida is the story of the love of two kings' daughters, Amneris and Aida, (whose fathers are at war) for Ramades, a young army commander. The story and setting are spectacular, and give ample opportunity for Verdi to write splendid music to match. Most famous of all is the triumphal music to celebrate the Egyptian victory over the Ethiopians, which, with its chorus and trumpet fanfares, is magnificent.

The quality of the music is consistently high, and Verdi provides, as a contrast to the celebrations, great delicacy in the music of the lovers. Another tragic ending.

Il trovatore has a plot too complicated to explain in full, and it is the dramatic music that has made it such a favourite. Set in Spain during the Civil War, it is the tale of two brothers who do not know they are related and who both love the same woman, Leonore, the daughter of a vengeful gypsy. This is a real blood and guts opera, most famous for the *Anvil Chorus*, the *Soldiers Chorus*, and the abortive marriage scene. As you will now expect, it has a tragic conclusion.

Falstaff is completely different from any other Verdi opera. It avoids big tunes and instead blends themes into a musical canvas reminiscent of Wagner's style. It takes more concentration on the part of the listener than Verdi's other operas, but it is worth it. A comic opera, it is a great experience live in the opera house, with both hilarious and magical moments. In many ways, it is to Verdi operas what the late quartets are to Beethoven – glorious flowerings of a genius in his last years, employing all his creativity and experience, and needing a few years before his friends caught on to his developments.

I leave you to explore the remaining Verdi operas at your leisure, and at your own pace. The trail should perhaps follow a route such as: *La Forza del Destino* (The Force of Destiny); *Un Ballo in Maschera* (A Masked Ball); *Nabucco*; *Simon Boccanegra*; *The Sicilian Vespers*; *Macbeth*; *Ernani*; *Stiffelio*; *Luisa Miller*.

9

BRUCKNER

Bruckner *His Life*

Joseph Anton Bruckner was born on September 4, 1824, in Ansfelden, near Linz in Upper Austria. His father, also named Anton, was a schoolmaster and a keen musician. He was the church organist, and his wife, Therese, sang in the church choir, so the young Anton was brought up on church music. He was the eldest son, and had ten brothers and sisters, of whom four survived infancy. Money was scarce.

Bruckner's musical education started early. His father taught him the violin and piano, and by the time he was ten he was good enough on the organ to deputise for his father. Occasionally he would be taken to services at the ancient monastery of Saint Florian, ten miles from Linz. A baroque structure of great splendour, which included a beautiful church containing three organs (of which one was particularly magnificent), St. Florian was a profound influence on the young Bruckner.

At the age of 11, Bruckner went to stay with his 21-year-old cousin and godfather, Johann Weiss, another schoolteacher and organist, in the nearby town of Hörsching. Weiss also composed, and he was able to broaden his young cousin's education substantially during the 18 month stay.

When Bruckner's father fell ill, however, he had to return to Ansfelden to deputise for him. After his father's death in 1837, his mother was determined that Bruckner's education shouldn't suffer, and she arranged for his admission as a chorister at St. Florian. He continued his education and music studies for the critical three years of his adolescence in this lovely setting, and St. Florian became his spiritual home, to which he often returned during his life.

Bruckner left in 1840 and trained as a teacher in Linz, following in his father's footsteps rather than pursuing music, but he continued to study music and heard works by Mozart, Beethoven and Haydn. After

Anton Bruckner

qualifying, it was off to an appointment in a small village near the Bohemian border as an assistant schoolmaster – a thankless existence, but he soon transferred to a more congenial village, and after three more years, in 1845, he went back to St. Florian as a teacher. All this time he had kept up his music studies, composing, and developing his skills as an organist.

Bruckner spent ten years teaching at St. Florian, and his duties left him ample opportunity to devote time to music. The death of a friend, Franz Sailer, in 1848 created the motivation to write his first significant work, a Requiem. Sailer left him an excellent grand piano on which Bruckner was to compose for the rest of his life. He was appointed organist at St. Florian in 1851, and some further significant choral works were produced over the next few years.

The slow transformation from teacher to composer continued. Bruckner visited Sechter at the Vienna Conservatory in July 1855 (the same Sechter whom Schubert had approached for lessons at the end of his life) and he was taken on as a pupil. Sechter also advised Bruckner to leave St. Florian, and later that year Bruckner was appointed organist at Linz Cathedral. By this stage, he was an outstanding performer on the instrument.

Over the next five years Bruckner, now in his thirties, devoted his free time to his studies in harmony and counterpoint through correspondence with Sechter. He composed little until he had completed his course. In 1861, he was examined by the top teachers from the Vienna Conservatory and obtained a diploma – Bruckner liked to have proof of his abilities. The highlight of the examination was his improvisation on the organ, which provoked the comment 'He should be examining us.'

Bruckner, still avid to master composition, now turned his attention to writing for the orchestra. He found a new teacher, Otto Kitzler, who was principal cellist and a conductor at the Linz Theatre, and a practical musician.

Kitzler undertook the first performance in Linz of Richard Wagner's opera *Tannhäuser*, and involved Bruckner in the preparation. *Tannhäuser* was a complete revelation to Bruckner, and gave him the inspiration he needed. He completed two un-numbered symphonies in 1864, and the *Mass in D minor*, his first major mature work.

In 1865, Bruckner received a personal invitation from Wagner to attend the premiere of his latest opera *Tristan and Isolde*, and due to delays in rehearsals he was able to spend some time making Wagner's acquaintance. Other composers he met around this time included Liszt and Berlioz.

Despite this wide exposure to sophisticated and mature composers, Bruckner maintained his own musical style. He composed his *First Symphony* in 1865–6 and his *Second* and *Third Masses* in the following two years. Now in his forties, he was clearly a slow developer, albeit a steady one.

His lack of self-confidence and gaucheness meant that he was unsuccessful in all his attempts to find a young wife (he had a liking for teenage girls) and was frequently rejected. He had an anxious disposition, was obsessive, and all the pressures caused him to have a serious nervous breakdown in 1867.

Four months in a sanatorium averted threatening insanity and restored his balance. The next year he was appointed to the Vienna Conservatory, succeeding Sechter who had died the previous year, and he moved to the capital where he was to live for the rest of his life. He was also appointed organist to the Imperial Court, on a provisional basis.

His prowess on the organ led to recitals in France, where he played in the Cathedral of Notre Dame before an audience that included the French composers Gounod, Franck and Saint-Saëns, and in London, where he performed at the Albert Hall in August 1871. He was acclaimed everywhere for his recitals which largely consisted of his own improvisations. Very regrettably, Bruckner did not write down any of these inspirations, and we are left with no significant works for the organ.

Successful performances of the most recent masses enhanced his reputation, but Bruckner now concentrated on writing symphonies. Today his unique style puts him amongst the great symphonists, but this individuality created much resistance in his lifetime, which in turn led to a much smaller output than might have been. We can only conjecture what great symphonies we might have had if Bruckner had been fully appreciated in his maturity.

Bruckner travelled to Bayreuth to show Wagner his *Second* and *Third Symphonies* in 1873, and to offer a dedication to Wagner. The *Third*, in its original form, included numerous quotations from *Tristan and Isolde*. After Wagner had accepted 'with immense pleasure' the story goes that they had some beers. Bruckner, altogether overwhelmed, couldn't remember the next morning which symphony was to be dedicated to Wagner, so he sent him a note saying 'Symphony in D minor where the trumpet begins the theme? Anton Bruckner'. Wagner returned it, writing underneath 'Yes! Yes! Best Wishes. Richard Wagner'. Bruckner referred to the work afterwards as the *Wagner Symphony*, not an astute political move in Vienna.

Bruckner became perceived there as a Wagnerian. Musical Viennese, a notoriously bitchy lot, were divided into Brahms supporters (traditionalists) and Wagner supporters (the New School) with the establishment firmly in support of Brahms. Achieving performances of Bruckner's symphonies became nigh on impossible. The Vienna Philharmonic considered *No.1* 'wild and daring', *No.2* 'nonsense' although it was acclaimed when performed, and *No.3* 'unperformable'.

An intense burst of creativity between 1873 and 1876 produced the *Third, Fourth and Fifth Symphonies*, an exceptional achievement. In just a few years Bruckner had become a master symphonist, since the *Fifth* ranks amongst the truly great by any composer. The tragedy is that Bruckner never heard it!

Well-meaning but ill-advised friends got to work on Bruckner to make his symphonies more acceptable – shorter (cuts were made) and less difficult to play (revised orchestration). Bruckner was extremely reluctant, but acceded. It totally undermined his self-confidence, as did the arrogant and extremely hostile reviews written by the music critic, Eduard Hanslick, a devotee of Brahms.

Bruckner, meanwhile, continued to teach at the University of Vienna, and gradually became a significant force in the city's musical life. He was a focal point for many young students, including Gustav Mahler, who many years later was to finance the publication of Bruckner's music out of his own composing royalties.

The premiere of the *Third Symphony* by the Vienna Philharmonic in 1877 was a disaster: most of the audience left before the end. Bruckner spent his composing time revising the *Third* and *Fourth Symphonies*, and didn't gain the confidence to start a new work until 1879. He completed the *Sixth Symphony* in 1881, and quickly followed it with the *Seventh*, the work that was, at last, to achieve recognition for him. Wagner died as Bruckner was completing the Adagio, and in the ending of this magnificent movement he added a moving postlude to the memory of his hero. No composer has had a greater musical epitaph.

The *Seventh Symphony* had its first performance in Leipzig in 1884 and was an enormous success, the ovation lasting for 15 minutes. A review of the concert captures the composer most movingly:

> One could see from the trembling of his lips and the sparkling moisture in his eyes how difficult it was for the old gentleman to suppress the deep emotion that he felt. His homely, honest countenance beamed with a warm inner happiness such as can only appear on the face of one who is too good-hearted to give way to bitterness even under the weight of most crushing circumstances. Having heard his music, and now seeing him in person, we asked ourselves in amazement 'How is it possible that he could remain so long unknown to us?'

Bruckner asked the Vienna Philharmonic not to perform the work, for fear of local criticism stopping his growing fame, but his fears were unfounded. His music gained increasing performances, particularly the *Seventh Symphony* and the *Te Deum*, which he completed in 1884 and considered to be his greatest work.

But at a time when he should have become a venerated and successful composer, there were still troubles ahead. His mighty *Eighth Symphony* was heavily criticised by one of his main supporters, the conductor Hermann Levi. Bruckner, devastated, entered a long period of largely unproductive revisions of many of his symphonies. The only real improvement was a revised version of the *Eighth*, which was a great success. His *Ninth Symphony*, started in 1889, was never finished as a result of all the wasted time.

Bruckner achieved considerable recognition in his last years. He was honoured by the Austrian Emperor, given grants by the Government and an honorary doctorate by Vienna University. A group of private benefactors also looked after him financially. But his last years were basically lonely. He lived in a lodge provided by the Emperor and was looked after by a housekeeper.

On Sunday October 11, 1896, he spent the day working on the finale of his *Ninth Symphony* and walking in the beautiful garden around his lodge. He died peacefully in the late afternoon.

The Karlskirche in Vienna was packed for his funeral three days later. A wind band played the Adagio from the *Seventh Symphony*. Anton Bruckner was then taken to his beloved St. Florian where, so appropriately, he was buried under the great organ. Amongst all the great composers he has, perhaps, the perfect burial place.

Bruckner *The Person*

Bruckner, in the second half of his life, became a little portly. He was of medium height, with a prominent nose, and closely cropped hair that became white. He usually wore country clothes, often ill-fitting, and looked, and was, rustic.

He was a man of outstanding and simple integrity. He was intelligent, but very naive and lacking in self-confidence. He had no sophistication, and always retained the behaviour, dialect, and attitudes appropriate to the Austrian countryside where he was brought up. Unlike most people, he did not adapt to his changing environment, and herein lies his strength as a composer. He was to remain constant in character, whilst developing substantially as a composer.

Bruckner had a powerful ambition, sufficient to become a celebrated organist as well as composer. He was, above all, a devoutly religious man. His life was dedicatated to God, in a tradition that went back centuries in provincial Austria. All his music was written for his Maker.

His social behaviour could be ingratiating, often naive, as when he tipped the conductor Richter for a good performance of the *Fourth Symphony*. On the other hand, he developed considerable followers amongst the students at the University, with whom he must have related well.

His insecurity led him to take advice on his compositions that would have been best ignored. He, amazingly, needed the authority of diplomas to prove his skill in music.

Some of his foibles, also rooted in insecurity, included the obsessive counting of church spires, and the observation of exhumations (he was present when the remains of Beethoven and Schubert were re-interred in 1875). He was constantly looking for a teenage girl to marry, but his gauche approaches, particularly late in life, were a source of embarrassment and always failed.

Bruckner *His Music*

Bruckner's greatness as a composer was shown first in his choral compositions, with his great *Third Mass* being completed at the very beginning of his symphonic cycle. In this work and the much later *Te Deum*, the style of his choral writing closely matches his large-scale symphonic works, but in much of his choral composition the music is smaller scale, as in the unaccompanied short pieces, the motets. Although the choral works and symphonies might seem two very different lines of exploration, they show two sides of a composer whose integrity and consistency and religious belief are common to both. And the symphonies nearly always sound better in a cathedral than a concert hall.

Dealing with the symphonies first, they are characterised by full orchestral forces, large time-scales (55 to 85 minutes), dominating rhythmic motifs, carefully built-up climaxes with frequent use of a release of tension only to produce an even greater ensuing climax, profound slow movements, and great melodic beauty. In the hands of great interpreters they have a tremendous spirituality. Their steady, inevitable unfolding is not for those who are impatient or seek only an enjoyable sensation; rather they represent the ultimate expression of a profound belief in God through the medium of music.

To enter this spiritual plane, the *Seventh Symphony* is the best starting point. Opening with a glorious, long-drawn-out theme on the cellos, against Bruckner's hall-mark of tremolando (shimmering) strings, an epic and beautiful work unfolds. The first movement is majestic, and is followed by perhaps the greatest of Bruckner's many marvellous slow movements. A deeply moving and sombre adagio, it builds to a tremendous climax which is approached twice, but only reached the second time. It uses the same theme that accompanies the words 'let me never be confounded' in the *Te Deum*. The movement finishes with the moving postlude which Bruckner wrote on hearing that Wagner had died. The last two movements are shorter, and the symphony ends with one of Bruckner's great perorations.

The other very accessible symphony is the *Fourth*, also known as *The Romantic*. It has another magical opening, with a long-drawn-out horn call emerging from shimmering strings. The horn calls are accompanied by flutes, and lead into a devastating climax, with one of Bruckner's favourite rhythms PA-PA-pa-pa-pa-PA declaimed with enormous power by the trombones and tuba. This movement maintains terrific tension right to the end in a good performance. The symphony continues with a slow movement in the style of a gently sombre funeral march, followed by a dramatic 'hunting scherzo' with resounding horns filling the horizons as one imagines in medieval times. The last movement wraps everything up effectively, with the opening horn call returning in triumph.

After these two symphonies you will know whether you are attracted to Bruckner, and if you are, whether it is to his lyrical or his powerful side. If you prefer the lyrical aspect then the next choice should be the *Sixth*.

The *Sixth* is different from Bruckner's other symphonies. This is not an epic, but a very attractive, almost pastoral work, which deserves more performances than it gets. The ending of the first movement has a marvellous flow and sense of inevitability, as does the slow movement. The scherzo is great one: it spins along alternating delicacy with great power, and it has an exquisite interlude in its middle section. The finale is a match for what has gone before – Bruckner at his most confident and fast-moving. The end brings the house down!

The *Third* is a highly dramatic work in D minor, starting with the strong rhythmic motif – PA-PA-pa-PA-on the trumpets, as described to Wagner. The first movement is fast-moving for Bruckner, and very exciting. A beautiful slow movement is followed by a typical Bruckner scherzo, and a last movement that teases the listener many times before finally releasing the opening theme into the triumphant major key in a glorious blaze of trumpets.

The mighty Bruckner symphonies are the *Fifth*, *Eighth* and *Ninth*, the latter two being cosmic in vision. The *Fifth* is an exalting experience, but it is of this world. A slow and mysterious introduction, punctuated by the brass section, leads into a powerful first movement with the PA-PA-pa-pa-PA rhythmic motif matched by a lovely melody. Following a beautiful, but not climactic adagio, and a highly original scherzo, the last movement of this symphony is a tour-de-force. It starts, like the last movement in Beethoven's *Ninth Symphony*, by recalling the main themes from the prior movements. It then sets off to combine initially two, then three, and in the climax, four main themes. If it sounds complicated in words, it is an enthralling and very tense experience in the concert hall. The last five minutes of this symphony are stunning.

The *Eighth Symphony* in C minor opens with one of Bruckner's most terse movements and is the only first movement where he ends quietly. The scherzo beats like a terrestrial clock, a relentless rhythmic theme shrouded in mysterious violins. It is followed by a profound and extended slow movement which, like that in the Seventh, builds up to a devastating climax. In the last movement Bruckner concludes triumphantly in the major key, combining themes from the previous movements and bringing an overwhelming experience to a triumphant close.

Bruckner never finished the fourth movement of his *Ninth Symphony*, but, like Schubert's *Unfinished*, it comes across as a perfect entity as it stands. From the tentative opening brass calls over quietly shimmering strings, the symphony makes clear that it is dealing with cosmic and spiritual matters. If the *Eighth* is mighty, this is quite awesome, not least in the scherzo where the orchestral rhythms have enormous power. The concluding slow movement, with hindsight, is a profound farewell to life. The parallels with Beethoven's last symphony (also No.9 and in D minor) are relevant: both symphonies speak at the same level.

Bruckner's first two symphonies are well worth hearing if you enjoy his music, although they are inevitably overshadowed by their successors.

As stated above, Bruckner's genius first appeared in his church music. These works are gradually becoming appreciated for their true worth, with many masterpieces amongst them. The *Te Deum*, for full orchestra, chorus and soloists, is a concentrated work lasting 20 minutes, and an ideal introduction, particularly if you come to it from the symphonies. Few composers could praise God with as much fervour as Bruckner, and the work is inspired. It builds to a great climax on *Non confundar* (let me not be confounded), and ends to the triumphant chant of trumpets. Bruckner's three Masses differ significantly from each other, and the *Second* and *Third* stand out. The *Third Mass*, known as the *Great*, ranks amongst the very best settings of the Mass, which is remarkable given its early position in Bruckner's output. From its very first bars it conveys its power, the fervent *Kyrie* is followed by an exultant *Gloria* with the full orchestra and chorus building to a great climax. The *Credo* matches the *Gloria*, and the music accompanying *Et incarnatus est* (and was incarnate) and *Et resurrexit* (and He rose again) is tremendous. The rest of the work continues at the same level, the *Benedictus* is particularly beautiful, as is the concluding *Agnus Die* (Lamb of God).

The *Second Mass* was written solely for woodwind and brass accompaniment, and is thus austere in comparison to its successor. But it is a noble and beautiful work, with marvellous sonorities. Bruckner's *Motets*, short sacred pieces which are often unaccompanied, are little jewels. The *Libera Me* (Release me), accompanied by three trombones, was written when he was thirty, and it is a very moving work, as are many others, including *Locus Iste* (This place) and *Os Justi* (The mouth of the just).

After Bruckner's death a few disciples continued to fight for recognition of his music. In recent years his perceived stature has grown enormously so that this marvellous original is now, at last, ranked amongst the greatest composers.

C. Tchaïkovsky

10

TCHAIKOVSKY

Tchaikovsky *His Life*

Peter Ilych Tchaikovsky was born on the May 7, 1840, in Votkinsk, a mining town in Vyatka province in Russia. He was the second son of Ilya Petrovich Tchaikovsky's second marriage to Alexandra Andreyevra Assier, who came from a French immigrant family. Tchaikovsky's father was 45 when he was born, and he worked as a government official at the local mines.

Tchaikovsky developed as a precocious, highly sensitive, and demanding boy, who adored his mother. She found it difficult to give him all the attention he demanded, and Tchaikovsky attached himself to his elder brother's young French governess, Fanny Durbach, when she was hired by the family in 1844. Her four year stay was to prove a particularly happy time for him, particularly in retrospect, but his childhood was very much dominated by women. The first piano lessons were given when he was five, and he showed an immediate talent for music, and a great sensitivity to it.

Life for Tchaikovsky was traumatized when his father resigned his job for an appointment in Moscow that failed to materialize. The family moved house, dismissed Fanny, and set off on a frustrating journey, via Moscow and St. Petersburg, eventually ending up in a small town many miles east of Moscow. But the young Tchaikovsky was dumped en route in a new school in St. Petersburg before moving to the new family home and a new governess. Soon after, however, he returned to school at St. Petersburg as a boarder, which cut him off totally from his family until his father retired and returned to St. Petersburg in 1852.

Tchaikovsky's mother died in 1854, from cholera, another traumatic experience for the young boy. His grief led him to music, and be began composing as an escape from his misery. In the meantime his musical training continued in a low key way, without any evidence of latent genius.

At the age of 19, Tchaikovsky left school and took up a job as a clerk in the Ministry of Justice. But his heart was not in it, and he switched from part-time lessons at the newly opened Conservatory of Music, to full time study in 1863 – a courageous decision. He graduated in 1866, having developed his composing skills considerably under the tutelage of the director, Anton Rubinstein.

It was Rubinstein who suggested that Tchaikovsky be appointed Professor of Harmony at the Moscow Conservatory, which was run by Nikolai Rubinstein, Anton's brother. So Tchaikovsky moved to Moscow where he stayed with Nikolai, and joined a convivial group of teaching musicians at the Conservatory.

Tchaikovsky, who was homosexual, briefly flirted with the idea of marriage to Désirée Artôt, an outstanding visiting soprano performing in Moscow, but it came to nothing. His homosexuality, and the difficulty of relating intimately to women, was to be a constant burden and ultimately led to his death. The positive outcome of this inner conflict, however, was the sublimation of his emotional energy into composition.

His *First Symphony* was completed in 1867, after much revision based on criticism from Anton Rubinstein, and it was performed early in 1868 to considerable acclaim. Tchaikovsky was on the road to fame, and he was soon accepted by the famous Russian group known as 'the Five' (Borodin, Balakirev, Rimsky-Korsakov, Mussorgsky and Ciu, who had largely taught themselves to compose).

His first true masterpiece, the overture *Romeo and Juliet*, soon followed. Tchaikovsky now spent a lot of time with a close friend and wealthy pupil, Vladimir Shilovsky. He visited Paris, Frankfurt and Interlaken with him, and during the early 1870s, typically spent his summers on Shilovsky's estate.

Tchaikovsky spent much of his time writing music for operas, though at first with only limited success. He did win a major competition with his *Vakula the Smith*, first performed in 1876, which he inadvertently submitted a whole year before the closing date, but it was not a commercial success.

1874 saw the birth of the *First Piano Concerto*, with its now famous introductory theme. Tchaikovsky intended to dedicate it to Nikolai Rubinstein, but he was so scathing about it that Tchaikovsky dedicated the work instead to Hans von Bülow, the famous conductor. It had its first performance in Boston, U.S.A., in October 1875, and was the first of Tchaikovsky's works to achieve full international exposure.

In his travels the following year, he attended Bizet's opera *Carmen* in Paris, and its powerful, passionate and fatalistic aspects were to encourage him in a similar direction. He went on to Bayreuth for the first performance of Wagner's massive opera cycle, the *Ring of the Nibelungen*, and met Franz Liszt, the virtuoso pianist and composer. However, he neither met Wagner himself, nor appreciated Wagner's new creation.

At the end of 1876, Tchaikovsky commenced a remarkable relationship with a Madame von Meck – remarkable in the sense that it was conducted totally by letters. This widow – her husband had recently died of a heart attack after discovering she had been unfaithful – was very rich. Her husband had made a fortune constructing railroads and she travelled in her own train or coach, with her large family. She was persuaded to commission a work from Tchaikovsky, and the letters started, quickly becoming increasingly open and intimate, with the safety of a pact that they would never meet.

Tchaikovsky still had a fantasy that marriage would rescue him from his homosexual nature. Equally remarkable as his newly commenced relationship with Madame von Meck was his proposal to a 28-year-old woman – Antonina Milyukova – who wrote to him as an admirer out of the blue. She started writing frequently, and threatened to commit suicide if he wouldn't meet her. Like an idiot, he gave in, and shortly afterwards proposed marriage. During this time he was completing his *Fourth Symphony* and writing the opera *Eugen Onegin*.

Tchaikovsky almost immediately found it impossible to live with his new wife. After having a nervous breakdown, and making a feeble suicide attempt, he left her. She was mentally ill, and a disastrous match for the highly neurotic Tchaikovsky. She was eventually to end up in a mental hospital.

Tchaikovsky fled to Switzerland with his brother, Anatol, to recover from his self-inflicted trauma. Shortly afterwards Madame von Meck settled on him a substantial regular income to enable him to concentrate on composing. This led to the completion of the symphony and opera, and he then wrote one of his happiest works, the *Violin Concerto*, before returning to Russia in April 1878 to live with his sister's family.

He no longer needed his position at the Conservatoire, and resigned. His new lifestyle consisted of travelling around Europe when not composing at home. His wife occasionally appeared in his life, causing disturbances, until Tchaikovsky discovered that she had both a lover and a child.

In 1879 Madame von Meck sponsored the first performance of the *Fourth Symphony*, which was dedicated to her. It took place in Paris, but the response was lukewarm; Tchaikovsky's correspondence with her provided him with the next best thing to an intimate relationship, and the communications increased in intensity. Twice their paths actually crossed, once in Florence and once when he stayed on her estate in Russia and they bumped into each other by accident – to mutual confusion – but no words passed!

This nomadic existence was not good for Tchaikovsky, who produced only two recognized masterpieces over the next five years: the exuberant *Capriccio Italien* and the elegant *Serenade for Strings*. Perhaps the whole marriage episode required a long recovery, during which he kept away from works with great emotional content.

Tchaikovsky gave up his wanderings in 1885 and rented a house close to Moscow. Like Gustav Mahler was to do, he started a disciplined routine of composing during regular hours each day. His energies were focused on a new symphony, the idea for which had been given to him by the composer Balakirev, who suggested the subject of Byron's poem, '*Manfred*', and gave him a programme to go with it. Tchaikovsky was back into powerful, emotional composition again, and *Manfred* was completed in six months and first performed in March, 1886. Balakirev, its dedicatee, thought it Tchaikovsky's best work to date.

In 1887, Tchaikovsky managed to overcome his great fear of conducting an orchestra, and started a new phase of his career in which he personally introduced his works to the cities of Europe. It was on the first of his conducting tours that he had his celebrated meetings with Brahms and later Dvořák. His concerts were a considerable success and after his return in 1888, he completed his *Fifth Symphony*.

After another concert tour in 1889, he composed his marvellous ballet *The Sleeping Beauty* and started a new opera *The Queen of Spades*. But the following year he suffered a devastating and permanent shock in a letter from Madame von Meck. Using the excuse that she was in financial difficulties, she stopped his financial support and broke off the relationship. Fourteen years of great intimacy through letters, which had sustained Tchaikovsky both emotionally and economically, were ended. He took it as an enormous rejection, in spite of her closing words 'Goodbye, my dear, incomparable friend, and do not forget one whose love for you is infinite'.

In fact, Madame von Meck was very sick and had great family problems which she felt she had to devote her time to. It had always been a very strange relationship, though ideal for Tchaikovsky, but it was a truly sad ending, one that left Tchaikovsky with an emotional void that was never to be refilled.

A visit to the United States and the composition of the ballet music *The Nutcracker* rescued him from depression in 1891. Early the next year the 31-year-old conductor and composer, Gustav Mahler, took over from Tchaikovsky for the first performance of the opera *Eugene Onegin* in German, at Hamburg. Tchaikovsky immediately recognised Mahler's conducting gifts, referring to him as 'a versatile genius', and describing the performance of the opera as 'magnificent'.

At this point, Tchaikovsky became particularly close to his homosexual nephew, Vladimir (known as Bob), who was to be the dedicatee of Tchaikovsky's last, and greatest, symphony. Perhaps Bob filled some of the gap left by Madame von Meck.

Tchaikovsky was now one of the most famous and successful living composers. He came to England to receive an honorary doctorate of music from Cambridge University, and had 'a brilliant success' with his concerts. When he returned to Russia he completed his sixth, and last, symphony and gave the first performance on October 28, 1893. It was on the next morning that his brother, Modest, suggested the title *Pathetique*, which Tchaikovsky enthusiastically accepted.

Within eight days the great composer was dead. For many years it was believed that Tchaikovsky died of cholera from drinking unboiled water, but this was a massive cover-up for what was tantamount to an extraordinary execution. A member of the Russian aristocracy wrote to the Tsar complaining of the attention Tchaikovsky was paying to his young nephew, and the letter was given to the senior procurator of the Senate, who had been at the School of Jurisprudence with Tchaikovsky. He took it upon himself, concerned at the effect on the reputation of the school and its old boys, to set up an 'honour court', made up of himself and six other contemporaries of Tchaikovsky at the school. Tchaikovsky was summoned to appear before them on October 31, and they delivered their sentence. He was to kill himself, to avoid scandal.

Tchaikovsky, amazingly, went along with this. They had poison delivered to him the next day. Tchaikovsky took the poison and died early in the morning of November 6, after suffering appalling pain. 'Honour' was thus done, and Tchaikovsky was given a magnificent funeral service in Kazan Cathedral. He was buried at the Alexander Nevsky monastery, where Glinka, Borodin and Mussorgsky, Russia's other great composers, lay.

Tchaikovsky's death (or murder in moral terms) was a tragedy. He was 53, and would no doubt have composed many more masterpieces. News of his death shocked music lovers everywhere. The music of the *Pathetique* took on new significance and the symphony had enormous success around the world.

Tchaikovsky *The Person*

Tchaikovsky was of above average height and an impressive looking man. He had greying hair in his later years, blue eyes and a carefully trimmed beard. He dressed immaculately, and was sophisticated in his behaviour. He was also a highly neurotic person, constantly worried about his health and his interactions with people.

Brilliant, with a self-created genius for composition, he had a delicacy and sensitivity that were highly developed. He was also a homosexual, at a time when this was an unacceptable inclination. In the main he managed to hide his true personna from the people he met, although he sought wherever possible to avoid meeting people whom he didn't know. He usually managed to hide from them the claustrophobia he felt in their company.

Very intelligent, his sheltered upbringing in a female environment left him ill-equipped to cope with the real world. The women in his early life died or left him, and this may explain much of his anti-social and homosexual behaviour. He escaped whenever he could, whether into his music, his travels, or his strange relationship with Madame von Meck. He avoided intimate relationships except with very close male friends.

Tchaikovsky is a figure of some sadness on a personal level, but his music – which reflects his state of mind – was for him, and is for us, a major compensation. Very little in his life reflects badly on him, given an understanding of his nature, and he maintained his integrity rigidly to the fatal end.

Tchaikovsky *The Music*

The popularity of Tchaikovsky's music is fully deserved, as he created works with great tunes, beautifully and fully orchestrated, with plenty of excitement and passion when appropriate.

Start with the excerpts from the ballet music to *Swan Lake*, and you are immediately caught up in the best of Tchaikovsky, teasing out the marvellous possibilities of the symphony orchestra. With each short episode telling its own tale, this is highly enjoyable, even without the ballet dancers!

Move on to the deep passion of the *Pathetique Symphony*, and you launch in at the deep end of Tchaikovsky's music. The brooding slow opening is typical, soon followed by a marvellous, throbbing, andante theme. As this fades away, the orchestra bursts in with shattering impact, creating a great shock when you are listening at home and cannot see the players getting prepared, as you can in the concert hall. It is a marvellous movement. The second movement is in a swiftly moving waltz style, and it is followed by a brilliant march. This can seem like the end of the work, but the last movement, however, is a passionate, slow leave-taking of melting beauty and sorrow, which finally dies away to nothing.

The *Violin Concerto* is one of the great virtuoso works for this instrument. Extremely melodic, the solo violin is pitted against a full orchestra at times, but there is great delicacy and excitement in the violin score to contrast with the swaggering theme taken up by the orchestra. The quiet and serene slow movement is followed by a very lively finale, with a virtuoso violin display, and it ends in barn-storming fashion.

The *First Piano Concerto* opens with a world-famous theme, majestic and instantly memorable. Remarkably, Tchaikovsky drops this theme after the first few minutes, although at first hearing of the concerto its return is eagerly anticipated. The piano part is masculine and virtuoso. The first movement is episodic rather than classical in its structure, but it is consistently enjoyable, and has a splendid climax at the end. Like the *Violin Concerto*, there is a delicate slow movement of considerable charm. Starting slowly, it has an unusual and fast middle section before the music returns to the opening theme. The finale, as you will now expect from Tchaikovsky, is very exciting with a stunning ending.

The *Fantasy Overture, Romeo and Juliet* shows Tchaikovsky's early gifts in a dramatic and terse work. This first masterpiece, opening quietly, depicts the moods of Shakespeare's great romantic tragedy. The love theme is marvellous, pure and simple at first, but soon throbbing with passion. The ending is most poignant. Definitely one for lovers, of music or otherwise.

Tchaikovsky's other ballet scores, *Sleeping Beauty* and *The Nutcracker*, are long works, and selections of the music have been extracted to create suites of more accessible length. These are the best way into the music until you feel the urge to hear the rest. It is highly attractive music that doesn't demand such levels of concentration as the symphonies and concertos.

Another side to Tchaikovsky's art can be heard in the *Serenade for Strings*, a stunningly beautiful work in which the second movement, a waltz, is particularly well known. The writing for the strings is rich and many-textured, and the sound can be really gorgeous.

Tchaikovsky's symphonies are a very strong part of his output. They can be tremendously exciting, and his gift for melody is always there. He wrote seven altogether, although one – entitled *Manfred* – doesn't bear a number.

The *Fifth* is a brooding, very Russian work, and extremely evocative. After a slow introduction it develops into a driving allegro of considerable nervous energy. Melody and passion are here in abundance. The slow movement has one of the most famous horn solos – a moving lament – and continues the highly emotional mood of the preceding one. The movement climaxes with the return of the symphony's introductory theme. After a waltz, the finale is introduced with this same theme, now resolved in the much happier major key. The music builds up inexorably, and ends with a great climax in which the recurring (motto) theme is played in triumph by the full orchestra. It brings the house down!

Symphony No.4 is another motto symphony. It starts with a most dramatic statement of the theme on the horns. Tchaikovsky referred to the theme as 'Fate', and it appears throughout the work. The powerful first movement is followed by a gentler one, more melancholic than tragic. The third movement, the scherzo, is a tour-de-force, with the strings playing pizzicato (plucked) throughout – great fun. The last movement announces itself with full orchestra, including cymbals, in a very positive mood. The 'Fate' theme returns but is fully vanquished in an exhilarating ending.

Manfred is a symphony written to depict the hero of a famous poem written by the poet Lord Byron. It comes over as a very taut work, each part essential to the whole, and as though Tchaikovsky was determined not to be too flamboyant. Here is the essence of the programme that he used:

> *1 Manfred walks in the Alps, tormented by doubts, remorse and despair. Nothing can give him the oblivion he craves. Memories of the beautiful Astarte, whom he loved and lost, burn in his heart. Nothing can banish the curse that weighs down Manfred's soul, he is tortured endlessly by the most appalling despair.*
> *2 The Fairy of the Alps appears to Manfred in the rainbow of a waterfall.*
> *3 Pastoral. The simple, free, and peaceful life of the mountain people.*
> *4 The underground palace of Arimanes, the god of evil. Manfred appears as a riotous Bacchanal comes to a frenzied climax. He calls up the shade of Astarte. She appears, and predicts the end of Manfred's earthly torments. Manfred dies.*

113

The music is masterly and deserves to be more widely known and played, as it is in the same class as the *Pathetique*. Manfred's despair is heard immediately in the theme for bassoons and clarinet that opens the work in Tchaikovsky's favourite marking – 'slowly and lugubriously' – but past episodes in his life are depicted with passionate and colourful music in the rest of the movement. The second movement has a totally contrasting lightness of touch, scampering violins and harp, and there is a central section with a lyrical melody of great charm. The mood created by the pastoral movement is of a balmy summer day with all well in the world, except for the odd storm, until Manfred appears. The last movement is a fitting and exciting climax, with themes and orchestration providing brilliant images. Manfred's death is marked by the entry of an organ which leads a skin-tingling and moving postlude.

Tchaikovsky's first three symphonies are well worth getting to know after the last four. Although they stand in the shadow of their later brothers, they are very attractive and melodic works. The *First*, called *Winter Daydreams*, opens magically and confidently, has a beautiful adagio, a light-footed scherzo, and a great theme in the last movement. The *Second*, called *The Little Russian*, is full of folk tunes. It has a bridal march as the second movement, and a lively scherzo before a finale of considerable nobility. The *Third Symphony* is in five movements, the first jaunty, the second a lilting dance which is followed by a poised adagio. A scherzo which combines the scampering lightness of Mendelssohn with a Bruckner-like rhythmic motif is followed by a finale mainly in polonaise tempo.

The *Capriccio Italien*, in Tchaikovsky's words, is 'effective because of the wonderful melodies I happened to pick up, partly from published collections and partly out in the streets (of Rome) with my own ears.' This is so true, and it is a most exuberant and evocative piece. Close your eyes and you are in Southern Europe, with all sorts of magnificent pictures conjured up in your mind. Some of the time, however, I feel it could be Madrid rather than Rome!

When a composer's first piano concerto is a great hit and you know he wrote two more, great expectations are aroused, but it is only recently that Tchaikovsky's *Second Piano Concerto* – as a result of a great recording – has started to emerge from the shadows. It has an inspired slow movement where a solo cello and violin have the sad theme to themselves before the piano is heard. Tchaikovsky creates a magical mood throughout this extended andante. The outer movements are tuneful and rhythmic, thoroughly enjoyable, and they provide a good setting for the concertante central movement.

Tchaikovsky wrote many other attractive works, including the operas *Eugene Onegin* and the *Queen of Spades*, four *Suites* for orchestra, three string quartets and a string sextet called *Souvenir de Florence*, and various orchestral pieces such as the famous *1812 Overture*.

Antonín Dvořák

11

DVOŘÁK

Dvořák *His Life*

Antonín Leopold Dvořák (pronounced Durvorschak) was born on September 8, 1841, in the attractive small village of Nelahozeves, 20 miles north of Prague, in Bohemia.

His father, František Dvořák, was the local publican and butcher, and his mother, Anna, had been in service at the local castle of Prince Lobkowitz. Antonín was the eldest of eight children in this Catholic family, and money was scarce.

Dvořák's father played the violin and zither and sang, and the young boy was brought up amidst church and folk music. He learned the violin from the age of eight, when he started at the local school – luckily the schoolmaster was a good musician. At the age of 12 Dvořák was sent to learn German, the official language, at another school in Zlonice, a small town 20 miles to the west, where he stayed with an uncle.

The headmaster of his new school, Antonín Liehman, was an accomplished musician and taught Dvořák composition as well as the violin and organ. Liehman was the centre of Zlonice's musical life and he composed for, and directed, the local musicians in the orchestra which he organised. This gave the young Dvořák outstanding early experience.

His family joined him in Zlonice in 1855, but the move turned out to be a financial disaster for his father, as the new inn failed. The young Dvořák was boarded out for a year to get his German up to scratch and when he returned, his old teacher, Liehman, tried to persuade his father to send him to Prague to realise his musical gifts. But František Dvořák couldn't afford it and, furthermore, was determined that his eldest son should continue the family tradition and become a butcher.

Dvořák's apprenticeship as a butcher, a trade he hated, lasted about a year, during which time pressure was built up, particularly by Liehman, to switch the gifted youth to a musical career. With the help of Dvořák's uncle, it was finally agreed that he should go to Prague to study at the Organ School.

Dvořák travelled to Prague, accompanied by his mentor, Liehman, in the autumn of 1857, and initially took lodgings with a cousin. He was just 16. Amongst his fellow pupils his talents were unexceptional but he was thrown into a life full of music. He played the viola in the orchestra of the Saint Cecilia Society, an excellent band whose conductor was a lover of the music of the great operatic composer, Richard Wagner, although this 'modern' music was shocking many at the time. It was not the sort of music featured in the curriculum of the Organ School and Dvořák fell for it.

Dvořák stayed at the Organ School for two years, and graduated, second out of 12, as a qualified organist and choirmaster. The verdict on his talents at this time seemed to be that he was no prodigy, but rather a practical musician. He now had to make his own way in life.

So commenced the long period – 13 years – of scratching a living and developing his talents before he achieved recognition. He started off with free lodgings, earning money by playing the viola in a small orchestra which performed at restaurants and balls. This band was to become the nucleus of the opera orchestra which was formed in 1862, and Dvořák became its principal viola player. The next year, Richard Wagner conducted a concert in which Dvořák played. From 1866, the orchestra played under the emerging great Czech composer, Smetana, whose nationalistic music (Czechoslavakia was under Austrian control) aroused great enthusiasm amongst the people. Dvořák gained great practical experience during this period.

In these first years on his own, Dvořák also gave lessons – when he could get the pupils. He moved to share rooms with a group of friends where he had access to a piano, pursued his study of the music scores of the great composers and carried on his own efforts at composition. He was highly determined, ambitious, and industrious. He was also very self-critical, destroying most of his early compositions, and his first official work, Opus 1, was a string quintet written and completed in 1861.

In 1864, he fell in love with a 16-year-old girl, Josefina Čermáková, and wrote a song cycle, *Cypresses*, for her but she did not return his affection. The next year he composed his first symphony, *The Bells of Zlonice*. He didn't intend it to survive and it was only discovered early this century. Later that year he completed another symphony which had to wait until 1888 for its first performance.

Under the influence of Smetana and Wagner, Dvořák turned to operatic composition, ultimately devoting many years to it, but his operas were to be his least successful works. *Alfred* was composed in 1870, and he followed it up with another opera the following year.

Dvořák's breakthrough came in 1873. The previous year he completed a patriotic cantata *Hymnus: The heirs of the White Mountain*, and its premiere brought the great success he needed. He also wrote his first mature symphony, *No.3*, in 1873, and this won him an Austrian State Prize the following year and brought him to the attention of Brahms – the start of a long and supportive relationship. Dvořák was to get further grants for several years from the Austrian State Commission.

Dvořák married Anna Čermáková, Josephina's younger sister, in November 1873, and the marriage was to be a very happy one. They moved into their own home and Dvořák gave up his job as a viola player for a position as a church organist. He completely re-wrote the music for his second opera and it had a successful first performance in November 1874.

The death of their baby daughter the next year inspired him to compose a setting of the *Stabat Mater* (The Mother weeps) in memory of her. Soon after, he composed a set of songs called *Moravian Duets*, and Brahms recommended to his publisher, Simrock, that he take them on. At last Dvořák's music was to be heard and earn him money outside Czechoslovakia. By now he was composing a steady stream of excellent works, including the *Serenade for Strings* and the *Fifth Symphony*.

He gave up his church organist's position in 1877 to devote himself entirely to composing, but tragedy struck with the deaths, within a month, of his second daughter and his three-year-old son. Dvořák completed the setting of the *Stabat Mater*, a choral work which was to be a great success, now dedicated to the memory of his three children. He still persisted in opera writing, and his sixth opera, *The Cunning Peasant* was performed in early 1878.

119

The *Slavonic Dances* were commissioned by Simrock in the same year, and in December, Dvořák took the train (he was an avid train-spotter) from Prague to Vienna to meet Brahms for the first time and to present the score of a quartet dedicated to him.

Dvořák was now conducting his own music and as his fame spread, he started to travel. At last he was earning some decent money too as he negotiated higher fees for his compositions. Dvořák's needs were simple: he loved to compose, to get out into the country and to be with his family. After their early tragedies, Dvořák and his wife eventually had a large family – daughters Otilie, Anna, Magda, and Aloisie and sons Antonín and Otakar.

By 1878, Dvořák was producing great works consistently, and this continued for the rest of his life (he also wrote a lot of money-spinning smaller pieces). The death of his mother, in 1882, was a heavy blow and drew from Dvořák one of his finest chamber works, the *Piano Trio in F minor.*

His popularity in England, particularly through the *Stabat Mater*, led to an invitation and he arrived in London in March 1884, to a great reception. He conducted the *Stabat Mater* at the Albert Hall with nearly a thousand performers and was acclaimed as never before in his life. His other concerts reinforced the love affair with England and Dvořák was to return four more times before the end of 1885. The young Edward Elgar played under Dvořák in a performance of the *Sixth Symphony*, in September 1884, at the Three Choirs Festival, and wrote afterwards to a friend 'I wish you could hear Dvořák's music. It is simply ravishing . . .'

On his return from the first visit to London, Dvořák realised a dream and bought a plot of land in the country, on which to build his own cottage. This was on the estate of his sister-in-law's husband, Josephina having married a count, no less. Dvořák was to spend most of his summers there for the rest of his life, close to nature and rearing pigeons (he was a pigeon-fancier as well as a train-spotter).

His next major work was the *Seventh Symphony*, which he first performed in London in April 1885, to great acclaim. Leeds saw the premiere of a new Oratorio, *Saint Ludmilla*, in October. He wrote home: 'It went off gloriously.. . . the enthusiasm was such as I have not experienced in a long while! I confess that I have never before been so strongly moved.'

Over the next few years, Dvořák conducted his works in Germany and Russia: the Russian trip was at the invitation of Tchaikovsky, who became a firm friend when he visited Prague on one of his own concert tours. By 1890, Dvořák was internationally famous; he was receiving honours from many parts of Europe (Cambridge University awarded him a Doctorate in Music); he was happy, he was well established financially and he was writing great music.

Dvořák took up the appointment of professor at the Prague Conservatory at the beginning of 1891, and became a highly valued teacher. But the main event of 1891 was an invitation to be the director of the new National Conservatory of Music, in New York. Mrs. Jeanette Thurber, the wife of a successful wholesale grocer, needed an internationally renowned musician to provide prestige for her venture. She made Dvořák an offer that he couldn't refuse – $15,000 a year (a fortune in those days), eight months in America for each of two years, ten concerts to conduct each year.

In September 1892, Dvořák, his wife and two of his children, set off for the United States, with a young musician friend, Josef Kovařík, whose father lived in Iowa. They arrived on the 26th, and Dvořák's first concert on October 21 included the premiere of his *Te Deum*. He settled down remarkably well to this vastly different culture, quickly moving to his own apartment and discovering the main railway stations. Steamships became a new interest after his transatlantic voyage, and Dvořák would regularly go on board ships in New York harbour.

He was particularly supportive of his black students, and developed a strong interest in negro music, in which he saw the same roots that in Czechoslovakia had provided him with so much inspiration. He was soon working on his *Ninth Symphony*, but he was working so hard at teaching that he had limited time for composition. He decided not to return to Europe in May, so he sent for the rest of his family and they all spent the summer in Spillville, Iowa, staying with Kovařík's father. Dvořák was again back in the country, among country folk of Czech descent.

Dvořák returned to New York in September. The new season saw the first of the compositional fruits of his time in America, with his

Ninth Symphony, now entitled *Symphony from the New World*, rapturously acclaimed on December 16. In May 1894, the family returned to Prague and then on to their summer home in Vysoká. Dvořák was given a great home-coming welcome in both places.

Half his last season's salary was still outstanding at this time, Mrs. Thurber having run short of funds, and Dvořák returned to America in October, for just one more season, the highlight of which was the premiere of his magnificent *Cello Concerto*. He had re-written the ending in memory of his sister-in-law, Josefina, who died the previous summer.

When he returned to live permanently in Europe, Dvořák was one of the most famous living composers. In February 1896, he and Brahms attended the Viennese premiere of the *New World Symphony* together, and the next month he paid his last visit to London. Dvořák also took up the relatively new form of the tone poem, rather than the symphony, for his orchestral works, following the path of the great piano virtuoso, Franz Liszt. Dvořák visited Brahms when he fell ill in March 1897, and was a torch-bearer at his funeral just two weeks later.

Dvořák was made a member of the Austrian State Commission and the Czech Senate, although he never attended the latter. He now devoted most of his composing time to opera. He completed *The Devil and Kate* in 1899, and *Rusalka*, his best opera, in 1900. They were both successful in Czechoslovakia, but failed to make any impact outside. To celebrate his 60th birthday, the National Opera put on a cycle of all Dvořák's operas.

It was at the premiere of his last completed opera, *Armida*, in March 1904, that his health started to give cause for concern. He was diagnosed as suffering from arterio-sclerosis, and he also caught a chill. On the first day of May he felt better and got up to have lunch with his family, but half way through the meal he felt ill again and had to be helped back to bed. He suffered a heart attack and was dead when the doctor arrived.

That night in Prague, the Opera House was draped in black and soon the whole country was in mourning for its great and beloved composer. Many thousands lined the funeral route four days later. At the church, part of his *Requiem* was played, and he was buried in the cemetery of Vsyšehrad.

Dvořák *The Person*

Antonín Dvořák was tall – about 5ft.10ins. – dark-haired, with a bushy beard and piercing eyes. He was of solid build. He was a man of great dignity and integrity but absolutely natural. He never lost the values and appreciation of his early countryside upbringing and was always happiest when he returned there and mingled with the locals. He remained natural and unpretentious, unsophisticated in the best sense, and modest. He was very loyal. He was, above all, a family man and very human. The family came first and his six children, in particular, were a great source of joy, although never erasing the memory of the first ones who died. He hated to be apart from them.

He was quite conservative and not a great innovator, choosing rightly to play to his strength as a melodist and his affinity with nature. His instincts were to be cautious. He showed his feelings only rarely.

His interests extended well beyond music but in unsophisticated, almost childlike pleasures – trains, pigeons, and ships. He clearly enjoyed and lived a full life with some determination. He was well-balanced and his ambitions were high only up to a point. In his last years, he was too content in his success as a composer and in the enjoyment of his family, to strive for even greater works and to take his art to a higher level. He was almost certainly the most normal of the great composers and he had his values well sorted out.

Dvořák *His Music*

Dvořák, with Schubert, was one of the world's greatest melodists, with a seemingly infinite capacity to write beautiful themes. His music is rich and positive, with pastoral flutes and woodwind prominent, full of the joy of life. But only occasionally does he allow his own deeper emotions to come through.

For the Dvořák 'Starterpack' I recommend the following works for an initial exploration of his different types of work:

1 Slavonic Dances The two sets, comprising a total of sixteen dances, are an ideal introduction to his music. Each dance is short, with an individual character, and they are all enormous fun with great tunes, rhythms, and superb orchestral sounds.

2 Serenades Two delightful works that follow on from the dances are the Serenades – the *Serenade for Strings*, and the *Serenade for Wind*, usually coupled together in recordings. The *String Serenade* has a lovely, lilting, opening theme. It is marvellously relaxed and relaxing, music, clearly written by a master musician. The *Serenade for Wind* is a very laid-back work, in which Dvořák's confident writing for the wind instruments is highly effective. The march-like last movement is particularly lovable, it exudes great vitality and humour. The ending, with whooping horns, is special. Mozart would have approved, I am sure!

3 Symphonies The logical next step is on to the symphonies. The *Eighth* breathes the same spirit as the works above. It is a lyrical and pastoral work and has a unique finale where Dvořák introduces his main theme at a slowish tempo, then later, and suddenly, brings it in at an exciting and much faster speed. This pattern is repeated and the ending is a stunning display of orchestral virtuosity, likely to make you jump to your feet cheering. Dvořák is a master of exciting conclusions.

4 Cello Concerto Dvořák's work is reputed to have inspired Brahms to comment that he would have written a cello concerto himself if only he had realised such a result was possible. It is an exceptional work, with a depth of emotion which Dvořák only rarely displayed. Compared with the Elgar *Cello Concerto*, which has been in the classical best-sellers charts for many years in the U.K., the Dvořák work gives little away in pathos and has the bright, optimistic openness of the full orchestra to provide a more universal attraction. Dvořák was undoubtedly influenced by his nostalgia for Czechoslovakia, and other personal factors. The lovely theme for the horn in the opening of the first movement, the musings of the slow movement and the revised ending commemorating his sister-in-law, are the high spots of a magnificent and enriching concerto.

5 Chamber Music The *American Quartet* took Dvořák just two weeks to compose. It has a glorious opening, with the distinctive first theme introduced by Dvořák's own instrument, the viola, over pulsating violins. Soon there is a contrasting second theme of melting beauty, as the energy is allowed to fall back – a superb movement. In the slow movement, a plaintive theme builds up a passionate intensity before dying away. An energetic scherzo is followed by a finale that matches the first movement for memorability. A bouncy opening introduces a catchy tune which leads straight into an even greater one at the same fast tempo. A slow interlude is soon interrupted by the rushing return of the opening. Dvořák slows down the second theme and wrings great emotion out of it within a few seconds, but then the music sweeps off to an adrenalin-creating ending.

Symphonies

Undoubtedly Dvořák's best known work is the *Symphony from the New World*. Completely different in mood from any of the others, it has justifiably captured the public's heart, helped by its unique title. His facility is the same as in the earlier symphonies, but it is as though he has used a different and more monochromatic orchestral palette. The Symphony itself – to me – captures the freshness of the 'New World' in a unique way. The first movement has great momentum with its memorable themes, the second instills a mood of rapt tranquillity with its famous theme for cor anglais, the English horn. The scherzo has a lovely lilting melody, and the last movement is as strong as a rock.

Several of Dvořák's other symphonies are outstanding. The *Seventh*, which many people regard as his best, is a powerful, concise work: it is as though Dvořák decided to write a European Symphony rather than a Czech one. The symphony is highly dramatic, and has quite thrilling climaxes to its first and last movements. In between, there is a lovely slow movement, with passages for solo flute and horn, followed by a scherzo of definite Czech origins. At the end of the symphony there is a glorious modulation from the minor to the major key, bringing an exciting finale to a triumphant close.

Dvořák's *Sixth Symphony* is one of his greatest, and possibly the most under-valued symphony in the whole repertoire. The opening is magical, a simple yearning theme tossed gently between woodwind and strings. This builds up to a powerful climax and a great work is under way with a momentum which it never loses. A glorious adagio with, again, a theme of great simplicity and purity is followed by a wild and swirling Czech dance for the scherzo. A gentle opening introduces a sparkling and joyful finale, and scampering strings build up to another terrific ending.

The *Third Symphony*, although an early composition, shows Dvořák's maturity from the very first bars. It has an amazingly confident swagger in an opening theme of great passion, instant memorability, and vigorous momentum. If ever there was a clear indication of the potential of a great composer to be, this was it. The slow movement, based on a persistent march rhythm, is very attractive, and the last of the three movements is lively and jolly. This is a very exciting symphony which has been grossly neglected and underestimated.

The *Fifth Symphony*, Dvořák's 'Pastoral', has a delectable opening with clarinets and then fluffy flutes, announcing a catchy theme over the strings. The first three movements exude great joy of life, but after the rumbustuous scherzo, the fourth movement enters a more serious mood at first, only to end in barn-storming fashion. The opening theme of the symphony returns on the trombones in triumph in the last bars. WOW!

Chamber music

Dvořák was also a marvellous composer of chamber music. The *Piano Quintet* is lyrical, quite beautiful, and brings great intimacy to Dvořák's melodic invention. There are some heart-rending themes for the piano, violin, and cello which help to make it one of the great chamber music compositions.

Dvořák's *String Quintet* (Opus 97) was written just after the *American Quartet*, and is a worthy partner to it. The opening movement unfolds Dvořák's unique North American colouration and thematic creativity. Passionate, urgent, and lyrical, it dies away in a nostalgic mood. The scherzo comes next, bustling in its outer sections, intense in the middle. The slow movement has a moving theme and variations of outstanding beauty, and this marvellously warm work is capped by a finale of joyful and jaunty melodies. The exciting ending conjures the picture of Bohemians bowing courteously, then spinning wildly off into the distance. Fabulous!

Dvořák wrote some outstanding piano quartets, piano trios, and other, earlier quartets. As with Schubert, if you fall for his melodic genius you will find much pleasure in exploring these works.

Other music

Dvořák wrote three *Concert Overtures* that are also highly appealing. Longer than the *Slavonic Dances*, and with much wider content, they are ideal works to start a concert. *Carnival* is the best known, – a very festive piece, with tambourine and cymbals prominent. After the hurly-burly opening, there is a gentle pastoral interlude. The ending is such a great show-stopper that it might be better suited for an encore piece at concerts. *Othello* and *In Nature's Realm* are the titles of the other two overtures, both typical of Dvořák's style.

There is one symphonic poem that I want to recommend initially: *The Golden Spinning Wheel*, one of Dvořák's final compositions. It carries great passion in its themes. A delightful melody on a falling scale is transformed from a delicate suggestion into a climax of splendour.

The compositions described above give an introduction to this master of melody, but if you develop a love for his style, there are many more discoveries to be made, including the *Requiem* and the *Stabat Mater* and a Mass, concertos for the piano and the violin, the other symphonic poems, and the opera *Rusalka*.

Gustav Mahler

12

MAHLER

Mahler *His Life*

Gustav Mahler was born on July 7, 1860, in Kališt, Bohemia. His father, Bernhard, owned the equivalent of an off-licence, and had married Marie Hermann, who at 20 was ten years younger than him. Gustav was the second born, but the elder brother died early.

It was not a love marriage, though it produced 14 children altogether, seven surviving infancy, with Gustav the eldest. His father constantly maltreated his wife, Marie. The family was Jewish and Mahler received a typical Jewish education in the town of Iglau, to which the family moved soon after his birth, his father now running a tavern.

Gustav had a natural musical talent and played the concertina well from an early age. He started piano lessons at the age of six and his grandfather gave him his own piano. His father was anxious for him to become a musician and at the age of 10, Gustav gave a public recital in his home town. In 1874, his brother, Ernst, a year younger, died after a long illness, and this proved a great loss to him. The following year, his father took him to play for the professor of pianoforte at the Vienna Conservatory, who, recognising a born musician, accepted Mahler as a pupil.

Mahler's fellow students and friends at the Conservatory included Hugo Wolf – who was to become a great songwriter before going insane – and Hans Rott – a highly gifted composer who died at the age of 26, also after a period of mental illness. They formed a highly intelligent, intellectual and closely knit group and became admirers and friends of the great (but generally unappreciated) Austrian composer, Anton Bruckner. They were also admirers of Richard Wagner, whose operas were then derided in Vienna by the pro-Brahms faction.

Mahler completed his course at the Conservatory in 1878, winning prizes for both composition and piano. For an understanding of his state of mind at this time – and it changed little throughout the rest of his life – an excerpt from a letter written in June 1879 is relevant:

The greatest intensity of the most joyful vitality and the most consuming yearning for death dominate my heart in turn, very often alternate hour by hour – one thing I know: I can't go on like this much longer! When the abominable tyranny of our modern hypocrisy and mendacity has driven me to the point of dishonouring myself, when the inextricable web of conditions in art and life has filled my heart with disgust for all that is sacred to me – art, love, religion – what way out is there but self-annihilation? Wildly I wrench at the bonds that chain me to the loathsome, insipid, swamp of this life and with all the strength of despair I cling to sorrow, my only consolation. Then all at once the sun smiles upon me – and gone is the ice that encased my heart, again I see the blue sky and the flowers swaying in the wind, and my mocking laughter dissolves in tears of love. Then I needs must love this world with all its deceit and frivolity and its eternal laughter.

Mahler devoted his time to composition, whilst earning money by giving piano lessons. He worked on a dramatic cantata, *Das Klagende Lied* (the Song of Lament), the text of which he wrote himself, but which was influenced by '*Des Knaben Wunderhorn*' (The Youth's Magic Horn), a famous anthology of German folk stories/poems which were published in the early 19th century and came to be a major source of Mahler's musical inspiration. He completed the cantata in 1880, and entered it for the Beethoven Prize, but it was rejected by the jury, which included Brahms.

Mahler's career, under the necessity of making money, took a dramatic new direction, to conducting. He came to excel at this, to the point of being arguably the greatest interpreter of music the world has yet seen. The years from 1880 to 1886 were taken up in learning the art of conducting in a variety of theatres. He started with musical comedies, but such were the ways and traditions in that part of Europe, where even small towns had ambitious opera repertoire, that he was soon conducting Mozart, Verdi and Wagner.

He had several love affairs during this time, almost always involving his leading female singer. For one of these, Johanna Richter, he wrote his first really mature work *Lieder eines fahrenden Gesellen* (Songs of a Wayfarer).

Mahler was very ambitious as a conductor. Demanding extremely high standards from himself, his singers, and his musicians, he aimed for the State Opera in Vienna. His reputation grew steadily and he achieved his first major appointment at Leipzig in 1886. Here he first met the young Richard Strauss, already becoming known as a composer, and a friendship started which was to last for the rest of his life. It was at this time that he began composing his first symphony.

Life at Leipzig was difficult – politics and rivalry complicated his work at the opera – and Mahler resigned in 1888. He was soon offered a 10–year contract at the Budapest Opera, where he had full commercial and artistic control. In 1889, his father, mother and eldest sister all died, and he became head of his family. He brought his sister, Justine, with whom he had an unusually close relationship, to Budapest to look after his home. He gave the premiere of his *First Symphony* in November not long after his bereavement but it had a poor reception.

Life in Budapest soon became difficult too (it was a pattern repeated due to the composer's demanding nature) and Mahler was dismissed in 1891, receiving very substantial compensation. He went straight to Hamburg as chief conductor, and here at last he enjoyed a period of stability – staying in Hamburg for six years.

Mahler quickly established a powerful reputation as a great conductor and he, at last, had musicians and singers worthy of his interpretations. Hamburg had a very famous old conductor, Hans von Bülow – whose wife had deserted him for Richard Wagner – directing the symphony concerts. He considered Mahler equal to the best, and gave him his full support.

In 1892, Mahler made his only trip to England, conducting Wagner's opera *Tristan and Isolde*, and Beethoven's *Fidelio* to great acclaim. He was now at work on a second symphony, and in 1893 started a custom that was to enable him to achieve a steady output of great compositions over many years. This custom was to spend the summer months in the countryside by a lake. He would take himself off to a cabin on the lakeside and work from early morning to mid-afternoon.

In 1893, this holiday resulted in the revision of his *First Symphony* into its final form. The next year he completed his *Second Symphony* – the *Resurrection*. His long search for a fitting conclusion to this symphony had ended at Hans von Bülow's funeral earlier that year when he had been powerfully moved by Klopstock's hymn *Aufersteh'n* (Resurrection).

1895 was a year of depths and heights for Mahler. His 21-year-old brother, Otto, whom Mahler considered more musically gifted than himself, though lacking self-discipline, committed suicide by shooting himself. And he had to undertake a doubled workload when his deputy left the opera unexpectedly. However, the first performance of his *Resurrection Symphony* with the Berlin Philharmonic was an outstanding success and when a gifted young soprano, Anna von Mildenburg, joined the Hamburg Opera, he fell in love.

By now Mahler was ready to take on Vienna, and started the necessary subtle moves to bring this about. The Viennese appointment was highly political, and open only to Catholics. Mahler, who had long since ceased to be a practising Jew, was ready to be baptized as a Catholic convert, and this took place in 1897. Mahler's formidable reputation, coupled with the need to upgrade the performances at the Vienna State Opera, combined to secure him the position, which is still regarded as the most prestigious of all conducting posts.

His *Third Symphony* now complete, Mahler decided to end his relationship with Anna. Leaving her behind, he moved to Vienna, giving his first performance at the Vienna Opera with Wagner's opera *Lohengrin* on May 11, 1897.

Mahler gradually breathed new life into the Vienna Opera, replacing most of the orchestra and singers. The wind of change blew through the opera house. Production standards (lighting, staging) reached brilliant and radical levels since Mahler was interested in the total impact of the operatic experience. Mahler became second in fame only to the Austrian Emperor, given the importance of his position, and music, to the Viennese.

Mahler was appointed Conductor of the Vienna Philharmonic Orchestra as well in 1898, but this self-governing group, whose players also made up the Opera orchestra, made life difficult for Mahler and he did not apply for re-election in 1901. Anti-semitism had reared its head.

Mahler's composing suffered in his early Viennese years. But in 1899 he bought land to build his necessary summer chalet by a lake in Corinthia, and during his summer break he began his *Fourth Symphony*, which he completed in 1901.

Although Anna von Mildenburg had by now joined the Vienna Opera, where she was a great success, Mahler had made it quite clear to her that the affair was over. In November 1901, at a dinner party, he met Alma Schindler, a remarkably beautiful and talented 22–year-old music student who, with her mother, moved in Viennese artistic circles. Her father, an artist, had died nine years previously.

They were engaged within three weeks, two days after Mahler's first performance of his *Fourth Symphony* in Munich. Their marriage in March 1902 caused quite a stir because of the age gap. Alma was a strong-minded and artistically ambitious young woman, very sensual and particularly attracted to creative men. But Mahler insisted she give up her independent activities, including her considerable composition talent, for him. Their first child, Maria (nicknamed Putzi) was born in November that year.

The *Third Symphony* was given its first performance in Krefeld in June 1902 and was a success. The next year it had another performance when Mahler conducted the Amsterdam Concertgebouw Orchestra for the first time. The response was overwhelming, and Mahler the composer was confirmed on the road to success.

The *Fifth Symphony* was completed during Mahler's first married summer in his chalet – he composed, while Alma wrote out the clean copy. After composition they would walk, swim, take a boat on the lake and relax in the sun.

The next summer Mahler finished two movements of the *Sixth Symphony*. This was completed the following summer by which time a second daughter had arrived, Anna. At this time Mahler also set two more of the poems by Rückert that mourn the death of children, making five in all. The sombre nature of his 1904 output was echoed by the last movement of the *Sixth Symphony*. When he first played this symphony to Alma, they were both reduced to tears, particularly by the three hammer blows in the last movement, which Mahler described as the last three blows of fate, falling on the hero, the last of which fells him as a tree is felled. These three blows and the completion of *Kindertotenlieder* (Songs of Dead Children) were to achieve added significance by events three years down the track.

Mahler's life was now a routine of opera, summer composition and European tours to conduct his own works, while his young family was left at home. His *Fifth Symphony* was first heard in Cologne in October 1904, *Kindertotenlieder* in Vienna in January 1905, the *Sixth Symphony* at Essen in May 1906. By the summer of 1906 he was well into the composition of the gigantic *Eighth Symphony*, the *Seventh* having been completed the previous year.

By 1907, Mahler's position at the Vienna Opera was coming in for criticism due to anti-semitism, increased financial deficits, and Mahler's absences to conduct his own compositions. After a vicious attack against him in one of the Viennese papers, Mahler decided he had had enough and resigned. Ten years is a long time to be in one place, and to direct the Vienna State Opera for that period was a remarkable feat. Over the years Mahler had received several attractive offers to go to New York, and now he was ready to go and take up the post of conductor of the Metropolitan Opera.

Mahler also had to face up to the news that he had a weak heart and must take life much more easily in the future. For a man who had, until then, been extraordinarily fit, undertaken a lot of strenuous exercise, and always driven himself to the limit, this was devastating news.

But worst of all was the death of his adored four-year-old daughter, Putzi, from scarlet fever and diphtheria. This tragedy, coinciding with the shock of the deterioration of his own health, aged Mahler dramatically. His life was never to be the same again.

Mahler bade farewell to Vienna with a performance of the *Resurrection Symphony* on November 24 and he was given an overwhelming ovation when the magnificent music came to its exalted close. Two weeks later, Mahler and his wife left Vienna by train for Cherbourg, en route to New York, where they were to spend their remaining winters, returning each summer to Europe.

New York's attraction was the money and the outstanding cast of singers attracted by money and each other: the great Russian bass, Chaliapin, and the Italian tenor, Caruso, were there. Nonetheless, the translation to New York of the essentially European Mahler, who was steeped in the great traditions of European music, was doomed to be unhappy.

Almost immediately, Mahler was embroiled in politics, for which he no longer had the stomach. When he refused to take on the vacant directorship of the Metropolitan Opera, the new director insisted on bringing the Italian conductor, Arturo Toscanini (later to become a legend in the United States) with him. On the concert front, Mahler was asked to revitalize the New York Philharmonic, on a three year contract starting in 1909, but his seasons with the New York Philharmonic were in his own words 'a losing battle'. His orchestra proved to be 'the true American orchestra, untalented and phlegmatic'.

The final behaviour of the committee of the New York Philharmonic Society, more than anything else, indicates what Mahler had to bear. The wealthy ladies who made up the committee summoned Mahler to a board meeting to justify himself. The heated arguments were secretly taken down by their lawyer hiding behind a curtain. Mahler had to give these ladies the final say in concert programming, and endure the most prejudiced criticism. Mahler conducted his last concert on February 21, 1911, in spite of illness, and sailed for Europe in March, a sick man.

The European summers from 1908 had maintained, unabated, the flow of Mahler's genius as a composer. In 1908 itself, Mahler and Alma spent a sad summer in the Dolomites, unable to return to their chalet and its memories of happier times. He eventually recovered some of his old spirit, however, as he completed his orchestral setting of poems with an oriental flavour, which was to become famous as *Das Lied von der Erde* (The Song of the Earth). The *Seventh Symphony* had its first performance in Prague in September.

The summer of 1909 saw Mahler working on his *Ninth Symphony* and giving some concert performances. At last he seems to have reconciled himself to his new physical limitations. The following summer he completed the *Ninth Symphony* and commenced the *Tenth*. During the summer, however, he discovered his wife was having an affair with a man half his age, the last thing he needed.

Through all this, he was preparing for what was to be the climax of his career, the first performance of the enormous *Eighth Symphony*. Because of the size of the work, and the large forces involved (it was quickly referred to as the *Symphony of a Thousand* because the first performance had that number of performers), it required much rehearsal. The two performances, on September 12 and 13, were magnificent successes, with the great conductor and composer cheered by audience and performers alike.

Mahler never conducted again in Europe. When he returned in April 1911, he was already dying. He became so ill that he spent his last days in a Viennese sanatorium, and died on May 18, 1911, during a thunderstorm. He was buried beside his beloved daughter, Putzi, under the headstone he had requested, which said simply

GUSTAV MAHLER

Mahler *The Person*

Gustav Mahler was 'thin, fidgety, short, with a high steeped forehead, long dark hair and deeply penetrating eyes' according to his protégé Bruno Walter. Others who knew him remarked on the prominent nose, the untidy hair, the large mouth and the strange walking gait in which he would regularly skip a step. He was very intense, if not fanatical, particularly where music was concerned. Mahler was highly intelligent, very intellectual, and – according to his wife's step-father – 'deeply, mystically instinctive'. His ambition and musical talent was exceptional, otherwise it would have been impossible for him, as a Bohemian Jew, to rise to become the Director of the Imperial Opera in his thirties. He also had great self-discipline.

As a conductor, he was able to extract great performances from orchestras through his will-power and unique interpretive ability, though he was considered despotic by some. His integrity demanded a constant search to realise the full potential of the works he conducted. He inspired admiration rather than affection in musicians, except those who became part of his inner circle – they became passionate disciples and revered him.

Mahler's life was driven by music and his standards of perfection. He was inevitably selfish as a result, and was often insensitive to the needs of others. He could, however, be the most delightful and interesting companion and he was also interested in other branches of the arts. He was chauvinistic (not that unusual at the time), insisting that his gifted wife give up composition, but he was also very human, open-minded and willing to seek help on personal problems.

He had enormous energy, both physical and nervous, and was extremely fit until his last few years, taking regular exercise. He has been described as neurotic and he was certainly highly strung, like many creative artists.

Mahler *The Music*

Mahler's music starts during the period of so-called late romanticism and stops on the verge of the modern movement. More than any other composer of this century, his music – 'encompassing the world' – seems to communicate to people of today, in spite of the length of his symphonies, which typically last between 50 and 90 minutes. Listening to the greatest Mahler symphonies can be an extremely emotional experience. Mahler can really get to you!

On top of this, there is a particular integrity in Mahler. In his music, whether it was conducting or composing, there is a quest for the truth and for the best, and this comes through in the music.

Mahler's music, because of the relatively limited number of works and their consistently high quality, offers you a rare opportunity to work your way through them chronologically, once you have decided that he is a composer that you like. This is offered as a thought, as it could be very rewarding.

However, his music is set out below on the same basis as the rest of the book, and the starting point is the *Second Symphony*, *The Resurrection*. From the very beginning you are gripped by high drama, as a powerful funeral march is introduced by cellos and double basses. This first movement is terse but builds to a great climax when the whole orchestra comes thundering down the scale, after which the opening theme returns. It ends by declining into an ominous silence. Two shorter and attractive movements build up a great sense of anticipation for the great drama ahead. The opening of the fourth movement – a contralto singing the beautiful Wunderhorn song *Urlicht* (Primeval light), which opens with the words 'O red rose' – sets in motion the magnificent finale in which the Day of Judgement is devastatingly depicted. Out of the total ruin comes one of the greatest experiences in music – the barely audible entry of the chorus singing *Aufersteh'n* (Rise again). From this moment to the end of the symphony there is an enthralling orchestral and choral build-up, with a very moving text, to an exalted and affirmative climax. Words are totally inadequate, do hear the symphony!

Des Knaben Wunderhorn (The Youth's Magic Horn) consists of 12 songs with orchestra. They have wide variety of subject, mood and orchestral sound, and a soprano and baritone share the songs, separately or together. *Reveille* is one of several of the songs that are anti-war, and it is given a sinister and ghostly accompaniment. *Where the shining trumpets sound* is another pacificist song, a soldier's moving farewell to his lover. Mahler's ability to create sadness, futility and despair is superb and these songs deserve wider popularity with their message, which is as powerful as a War Requiem. The lighter songs, such as *Rhine Legend*, provide sweet contrast between the delights of peace and love, and the horror and death of war. One of the greatest song cycles.

Mahler's *Symphony No. 1* is a very confident and highly original work, in which the composer has already found his unique voice. The opening creates an image of a bleak and eerie moonscape inhabited by birds, an evocative and pregnant introduction. The orchestra moves into a lilting melody, but the eerie mood is never far away. This first movement ends in stunning and abrupt style. A highly rhythmic and tuneful scherzo has a 'light music' middle section – a contrast that Mahler often uses. The slow movement is a funeral march based on the well-known 'Frère Jacques' theme – powerful, sinister and with macabre elements. The last movement explodes onto the scene and eventually builds to a triumphant ending, guaranteed to bring the audience, cheering, to its feet. It is a tour-de-force of orchestral virtuosity.

Symphony No. 4 is altogether a much gentler work. It opens with the sound of sleigh bells and a lovely melody and evokes a peaceful countryside. This makes the work particularly accessible. Mahler builds a powerful symphonic movement, disturbing the tranquillity, but the beauty is always there, and at the end the high violins create magical sounds. The second movement is a scherzo of a more macabre mood, but very delicate. Like the same movement in the first symphony, it has a middle section of light music. The slow movement is glorious, in the tradition of Beethoven's *Ninth Symphony* and Bruckner's great adagios. The strings again sound exquisite, particularly at the end when, with the harp, they hit the heights in a scintillating progression of chords. In the last movement, a soprano joins the orchestra to sing verses from the collection 'Des Knaben Wunderhorn', an idyllic song to end a lovely symphony.

Symphony No.5 takes us away from the influence of nature and 'Des Knaben Wunderhorn'. It opens with trumpet fanfares and a funeral march of great emotional power. The second of the five movements is also grief-ridden, but wilder. Between them, they produce a deep, despairing impact, and Mahler's mastery is total. The mood changes dramatically for the scherzo, full of Austrian waltz and country dance tunes – quite a shock in contrast. The fourth movement is the famous *Adagietto* as featured in the film '*Death in Venice*', and this is another of Mahler's great and very moving slow movements, with just strings and harp providing, again, strong contrast to what has gone before. Mahler closes this very personal symphony with a combination of new themes and ones used in the earlier movements to create a triumphant climax, miles away from the sombre opening to the work.

Symphony No.8, the Symphony of a Thousand, is the Mahler show-stopper, with its vast choral and orchestral forces. The scale and power of the work is announced in the first bars. The symphony consists of two parts, the hymn *Veni, creator spiritus* (Come, spirit of creation), and a longer section, the closing scene from Goethe's '*Faust*'. In the hands of a great conductor, it is an overwhelming experience. It is not an easy work to get to know, but emotionally it can be devastating, with the ending being particularly awesome.

Mahler's *Symphony No.9* is an absolute contrast to the massive scale of the *Eighth*. At the end of his life it is as if Mahler reverted to a chamber music clarity whilst still using large orchestral forces. The *Ninth* is a symphony demonstrating his expertise in breaking away from romanticism towards modern music. The first movement is marvellous in its cogency, delicacy and power. The second is deliberately brilliant and bizarre, like a dance of death. The third, a rondo burlesque, is a continuation of the style of the previous movement, but on a more humorous front. The crunch comes with the last movement, however. This is one of the very greatest adagios, and can send sensations right through your body – great music of love, leave-taking and nobility.

Das Lied von der Erde – The Song of the Earth – is at the same exalted level of composition as the *Ninth Symphony*. It is of symphonic scale and consists of six songs based on Chinese poems. The first five songs, sung alternately by tenor and contralto, (or baritone) are: *1. The drinking song of the sorrow of the Earth; 2. The lonely one in autumn; 3. Of youth; 4. Of beauty; 5. The drunken man in spring.* They each have great individual character and lead up to the marvellous, and extended, sixth song *Der Abschied* (The Farewell). This is Mahler's greatest song, with voice and orchestra combining in a most poignant adagio, which dies away with the repeated words '. . . Ewig. . . . Ewig . . .' (Eternally, eternally). In a famous performance after the war, the great singer Kathleen Ferrier was too moved to be able to sing these last words.

If you follow Mahler's music this far, here are some briefer comments on his remaining symphonies, which for different reasons I find to be less accessible, but which are still masterpieces.

The sketches for Mahler's *Tenth Symphony* have been turned into an amazingly impressive completed work, and only an expert Mahler musicologist would know that it was, in parts, a reconstruction. It is at the same inspired level as *Das Lied von der Erde* and the *Ninth Symphony*, and opens with a profound adagio.

Symphony No.6 (sometimes referred to as *The Tragic*) is a powerful, taut, and sombre work in four purely instrumental movements. It played an important part in Mahler's life and performances of it are usually a sell-out. The last movement contains the famous hammer blows.

Symphony No.3 is in six movements, each depicting an aspect of nature. The first movement is over 30 minutes long, and builds up to an extraordinarily rumbustuous climax. Mahler gave each movement a title; *1. Pan awakes, summer marches in; 2. What the flowers in the meadow tell me; 3. What the animals in the wood tell me. 4. What night tells me; 5. What the morning bells tell me; 6. What love tells me.* The fourth movement is a song for contralto, the fifth adds boys' and womens' choirs, and the finale is Mahler's first great adagio.

The *Seventh* (also known as *The Song of the Night*) is the least known. In its two outer movements, which enclose two eerie 'Nightmusic' ones and a central sinister scherzo, Mahler is unusually positive and not concerned with soul-troubling matters.

Mahler's main remaining significant works are orchestral settings of poems; *Lieder eines fahrenden Gesellen* (Songs of a Wayfarer); *Kindertotenlieder* (Songs for Dead Children); and the *Rückert Songs*. His early cantata,

Das Klagende Lied (The Song of Lament), is also an attractive work. They are all well worth getting to know when you are ready.

13

ARTISTS AND INTERPRETATION

*M*any great compositions have been explored in the last 10 chapters. The art of releasing the full impact of these musical scores is no easy feat and the subject of great performance and interpretation can be a source of heated debate, strong opinion and controversy among music lovers. An understanding of some of the factors that contribute to music making its maximum impact on you, will perhaps give you an added dimension in your exploration of classical music. It will also steer you clear of potential bewilderment and the purchase of recordings which, over time, you might find disappointing. There is certainly no need to settle for second best performances on cassette or compact disc.

Let me reassure you, however, that to enjoy and explore classical music, you do not need to become an expert on performance and interpretation: it is just helpful to be aware of the important part it plays. Each time a composition is performed, the experience is unique. There is always something special therefore about a live performance where, unlike on a recording, it is a one-off act of creation by the artists involved. To listen to music in the comfort of your home is marvellous and the ideal way to explore, but participating – because an audience is a part of a concert – is special. Wherever and whenever musicians gather to play music, whether they are expert or not, professional or amateur, young or old, few or many, a work of art is created afresh, and we can be a part of it. It does take a lot more effort than putting on a C.D., but it is worth it.

The greatest experiences in classical music are inevitably in the flesh, but are frequently captured for posterity in recordings that are the next best thing to being there. It is only possible to describe in general terms what can elevate a concert or an opera into a great experience, rather than an average or good one: the sense of rightness of the performance; the excitement; the commitment; singers and musicians singing or playing 'out of their skins'; the visual impact, particularly in the case of opera; the occasion; even the way you, the listener, feel; all these may play an important part. It is also useful to remember that one person's great experience may not be another's, and that is how it should be. How you respond is what counts.

One definition of a great artist in music is a performer who can become the medium of the composer and create in his audience a rare sense that 'this is how the music was meant to be'. Alternatively, he or she might give a unique perspective or insight into the composer and his work. An outstanding voice or instrumental capability; the phrasing of the music; the dynamics; the highlighting of key instruments; the choice of tempo; a deep knowledge of the composer; above all an understanding of the mood of the music, and the ability to convey it; these are some of the characteristics of great artists.

Music is also theatre, and some artists provide an added dimension through their personalities and idiosyncracies. Using examples of famous past and present performers, they might become prominent as:

- Superb virtuosos, like the pianist Vladimir Horowitz.

- Charismatic media stars, like the conductor Leonard Bernstein.

- Showmen, like the violinist Nigel Kennedy.

- Original interpreters, such as the conductor Klemperer.

- Creators of a beautiful sound, such as the conductor Herbert von Karajan.

- Fast tempo interpreters, like the conductor Toscanini.

- Elder statesmen like the conductor Gunther Wand.

- Heroes like the polio-stricken violinist Itzhak Perlman.

Not all those artists capable of giving great performances are famous, although many become so. One of the thrills of classical music is that sometimes you attend a concert, or hear a recording, of little known artists and suddenly realise that you are hearing a great performance. I once heard Beethoven's *Eroica Symphony* performed by a last-minute replacement for the scheduled conductor. It was magnificent and the little known, but highly experienced, German conductor was invited back to give a Bruckner concert. When the time came, I walked into the cathedral where the concert was to be given just as he was rehearsing the magical opening of Bruckner's *Romantic Symphony* and I knew immediately that he was one of the truly great Bruckner conductors, alongside Bernard Haitink and Gunther Wand.

The leader of the orchestra that night, a well-known and outstanding British musician, later described to me an exceptional concert that I had missed, conducted by a young British conductor. The violinist, who had played under many of the most famous conducting names of the past – Toscanini, Furtwangler, Klemperer, Karajan – spoke in the highest terms about the excitement of the concert, and the gifts of the conductor.

These are two examples to demonstrate how great performances occur in unexpected places to provide musical milestones in our lives and how great artists exist and are developing away from the limelight.

You may find over time, as you hear more and more great music, that some artists make music resonate more strongly with you than others. It makes sense to follow your preference of artists as you further explore classical music. It is at this stage that the world of pop and classical converge, and you can support a favourite star, whether it be a pianist such as Murray Perahia or Alfred Brendel, a conductor such as Simon Rattle or Gunther Wand, a violinist such as Perlman or Kennedy, a tenor such as Pavarotti or Domingo, and have the pleasure of hearing them in concerts as well as in recordings.

In my early musical development, the conductor Otto Klemperer was an important artist, for a variety of reasons:

- I discovered Beethoven through his now legendary recordings.

- The first concert I attended at the Festival Hall was conducted by Klemperer and introduced me to a life-long love of Bruckner.

- Klemperer had enormous integrity in his interpretations, solid as a rock in tempo, with no frills. The tension that he could generate resulted in some truly remarkable concerts.

- The sight of this tall (6ft.6ins), crippled, octogenarian disciple of Mahler being helped to the rostrum to conduct created an amazing sense of theatre and authority.

It is for you to decide whether, as you explore the music of the great composers, the favourite artists route or the alternative of taking each piece of music, and each concert, purely on its own merits, is the right one for you. What is certain is that all musicians who bring to life the works of the masters deserve recognition and support for their gifts. But those amongst them who have the greatest talent for communicating the full magic of music are special, as they are able to provide us with an added dimension of richness. The experiences that they give, whether in the concert hall or on disc, are ours if we want them.

14

BUYING RECORDINGS
OF CLASSICAL MUSIC

*I*n exploring classical music through recordings, you are presented with great choice. Some of the most popular classics have close on 100 alternative versions: on compact disc, cassette and long-playing record; perhaps played on original as well as modern instruments; analogue and digital recordings, and prices that range between £3 and £14. No wonder it can be confusing!

The ideal solution for selecting recordings of the music you have read about and decided to try, would be to find a list of specific recommendations in this book. Regrettably, the catalogue of current classical recordings is far too fluid for such a list to be valid for long. Apart from continual releases of new recordings, existing recordings are regularly being deleted, often to be re-issued at different prices and sometimes with other items included in the selection. Some recommendations would be out of date in the time it takes to publish this book, and many more would have suffered the same fate within a year's time.

In order to give you practical help in the critical task of making the right selections, let me take you through each of the matters of choice in turn.

1 CD, Cassette, or LP? Compact Disc (CD) is now the most popular format for classical music, and the strategy of the music companies is to encourage CD at the expense of tape cassettes and long-playing records (LPs).

LPs are relatively large, prone to damage and wear, and are unlikely to be around for long. Very few classical recordings are now released in the LP format, making it increasingly difficult for you to build a good classical collection.

Cassettes – the cleverly-packaged magnetic recording tapes – have the advantage of small size, portability and low cost (both for the cassettes and the players). They are prone to self-destruction in a faulty player, an annoying and expensive experience. Today, nearly everyone has access to a cassette player, whether in the home, a Walkman to carry anywhere, or in their car. Being able to listen to cassettes in a car is a great advantage for people who drive a lot. Not all classical recordings are issued on cassette, particularly boxed sets, but this need not be an inhibiting factor in building a classical collection. There is, however, an imminent new technology – Digital Compact Cassette – which is likely to appear within the next two years, implying the ultimate demise of current cassette technology.

CD has the advantages of an unsurpassable potential for the quality of sound, good packaging and documentation, long unbroken playing time, ease of use and relative indestructability. It is still more expensive than cassettes as a technology – the price to be paid for its superiority – but the price gap is shrinking. CD also offers easily the widest choice of classical music. If you do not have a CD player, I would strongly recommend that you acquire one, as prices have come down dramatically. CD is the ideal format for listening to classical music for the foreseeable future, it is an outstanding product which I recommend strongly.

2 Analogue or digital recordings? Compact Discs carry the initials ADD or DDD on their covers to identify whether the original tape recording was made with traditional (analogue) or digital (computer-based) technology. The full benefits of CD can only be obtained with digital technology, as this eliminates the possibility of background tape-hiss, allows the widest dynamic range, and enables perfect copies to be made. Digital recordings were introduced in the late seventies, and are now standard. However, there were many high quality performances and recordings made from the mid-fifties using analogue technology, and any tape hiss or dynamic range constraint – if detectable – tends to be insignificant compared with the impact of the performance. In a nut-shell, the differences can be very small, and – in my view – are much less important than the issue of quality of performance. That said, the combination of a great performance and an outstanding digital recording is the ideal.

3 Original or Modern Instruments? Increasingly in the last ten years there has been a vogue for performances on period instruments. These performances have aimed to reproduce the sound, scale and performing practice of the times in which the music was written. We, however, are conditioned to the relatively smooth sound and wider dynamic range of modern instruments, the result of technical advances over the centuries. Early attempts at these authentic performances tended to be off-putting – thin and sharp sounds, with scrawny violins in particular – but now, ensembles such as the London Classical Players and the London Baroque Soloists sound eminently acceptable, albeit different. There can be a special thrill in hearing the music as it was first heard, typically with enhanced clarity of the instruments, and the interpreters have also tended to give very lively performances. Original instrument performances are a welcome alternative to those on modern instruments for the works of Bach, Mozart, Beethoven and their contemporaries. I recommend that you try this style before too long to assess your reaction.

4 What recording and what price do you pay? Amongst the many recorded versions of each of the great classics usually lie a few that are generally recognised as truly exceptional, great performances, and I commend them to you. Luckily, many are available at bargain prices, since there is a tradition in the music companies that past recordings (which necessarily include most of the best interpretations, since only a limited number of outstanding performances are recorded in any one year) are usually cheaper than new ones.

The pricing of classical recordings can be quite confusing. The leading classical music recording company, Polygram, has four different prices for CDs, ranging from £6 to £14 in 1991. The enterprising label, Naxos, has its complete range at less than £5. You should take every advantage of the many situations where quality is high and price is low. With good advice and your own judgement, you can then build up a good classical collection at low cost. Where the outstanding performance of a work is at full price, you will need to choose whether or not it is worth the extra money. Only you can decide, but remember that a great experience is cheap at £14, if you can afford it.

5 Where do you buy the recordings? As you will probably have concluded, the successful selling of classical music requires a level of knowledge greater than for most products. Traditionally, this service has been provided by independent specialists dotted around the country and by some large stores in the West End in London. In the last year, the music chains and the multiples have woken up to the potential of classical music, and are addressing the challenge vigorously. In your exploration of classical music, you will benefit enormously from having a local dealer who can help you select the best value recordings of your choice of music. Let me give you some criteria for choosing a good dealer:

– Clear and up-to-date advice on the best-value recordings of the music in which you are likely to be interested.

– Breadth of stock such that he has most of your requirements immediately available.

– Willingness to make suggestions and to find, and order, any unusual requests.

– Friendly and knowledgeable service.

If you are unable to find a local service that meets your needs, let me suggest that you send for the Simply Classics Catalogue, a regularly up-dated selection of the best classical music recordings currently available, focused on value. This has been specially developed as a mail-order service for those of you who do not have access to a good source of classical music in your neighbourhood.

May your journey into classical music be enjoyable and long-lived.

APPENDIX 1

THE SYMPHONY ORCHESTRA

Usual formation

Horns	Percussion	Trumpets	Trombones
	Clarinets	Bassoons	Double Basses
	Flutes	Oboes	
Second Violins		Violas	
First Violins		Conductor	Cellos

Instruments of the Orchestra
Standard/ *Occasional*

Strings	Woodwind	Brass	Percussion
Violin	Oboe	French Horn	Timpani
Viola	Flute	Trumpet	*Cymbals*
Cello	Clarinet	Trombone	*Triangle*
Double-bass	Bassoon	*Tuba*	*Celesta*
Harp	*Contra-bassoon*	*Cornet*	*Piano*
Harpsichord	*Piccolo*	*Wagner tuba*	*Glockenspiel*
	Cor anglais		*Tambourine*
	Bass clarinet		*Xylophone*
	Saxophone		*Side drum*
			Gongs
			Bells
			Bass drum
			etc

APPENDIX 2

GLOSSARY OF MUSICAL TERMS

adagio Slow tempo.

Agnus Dei Last section of the Mass, 'Lamb of God'.

allegretto Quite fast

allegro Fast.

alto Low female voice.

andante At walking tempo.

aria Song.

baritone Male voice between tenor and bass.

baroque Elaborate music of period 1600–1750.

bass Lowest male voice.

Benedictus Section of the Mass, 'Blessed is he that cometh'

brass Term covering trumpet, trombone and tuba families of instruments.

cadenza Solo instrumental section of a movement.

canon Music where a theme is repeated to create overlapping between voices or instruments.

cantabile Singing style.

cantata Choral work, usually with orchestra.

chamber music Music of a scale to be performable in a room.

chamber orchestra Small orchestra.

chorale Traditional German hymn style.

classical Describes era and formal style of composition predominant in the last half of the 18th century.

klavier Early keyboard instrument.

coda Ending.

concerto Work for solo instrument(s) and orchestra, usually in three movements.

continuo. Accompaniment, usually on a keyboard instrument and using the bass-line.

contralto Lower female voice.

cor anglais Woodwind instrument, lower range than the oboe.

crescendo Increasingly loud.

Credo Third section of the Mass, 'I believe in one God.'

cycle Set of works to be performed together.

development Section of a movement (middle) where themes are transformed.

Dies Irae Section of Requiem Mass, 'the Day of Wrath'.

diminuendo Increasingly soft.

divertimento Light-hearted work for small number of players.

dolce Sweetly.

Dona nobis pacem Section of the Mass, 'Give us peace'.

Dorian mode Scale on white piano keys from D.

Glossary of musical terms

duet Combination of two performers.

ensemble A small group of performers or an operatic piece for several performers.

forte Loud.

fortissimo Very loud

forte-piano Early Italian name for the pianoforte (piano).

fugue Work where a number of parts follow each other at regular intervals in the same theme.

furiant Fast Czech dance.

Gloria Second section of the Mass, 'Glory to God on high'.

grave Slow.

impromptu Small work implying improvisation.

improvise/extemporise Play spontaneously.

Jubilate Psalm that opens 'O be joyful'.

Kapellmeister Musical director, originally master of the chapel- music.

Kyrie Opening section of the Mass, 'Lord have mercy'.

landler Austrian dance, like a slow waltz.

largo Slow.

libretto Text for an opera.

maestoso Majestic.

Mass Catholic religious service set to music, consisting usually of the Kyrie, Gloria, Credo, Sanctus and Agnus Dei.

metronome Mechanical and adjustable device for setting tempo.

minuet Dance in triple time used mainly in the 18th century.

moderato Moderate speed.

molto Very.

motet Short religious choral work.

motto Recurring theme.

movement Main and separate part of many types of composition, including the symphony, sonata, concerto.

octet Eight performers, or a work for eight performers.

opera Stage work with words which are sung to orchestral accompaniment.

opus A specific work.

orchestra A significant group of different instrumentalists, usually with a traditional mix between them.

orchestration The process of translating themes into the desired parts for each orchestral instrument.

overture Introductory orchestral piece for an opera, occasionally just a short orchestral work.

partita Set of variations.

Passion Musical setting of the story of the Crucifixion, traditionally performed at Easter.

piano Softly.

pianissimo Very softly.

pizzicato Plucked (strings).

postlude Ending piece.

prelude Opening piece.

presto Very fast.

quartet Four performers, or a work for four performers.

quintet Five performers, or a work for five performers.

recitative Type of singing half-way between song and speech, used to link sung sections of operas.

repeat Repitition of a section of music, according to the score.

Requiem Usually based on the Catholic Mass for the dead, set to music.

rococo Decorative and light style of music.

romantic More emotionally expressive style of music following the classical phase of composition, commencing with Beethoven.

rondo Composition in which a section keeps recurring.

Sanctus Section of the Mass, 'Holy'.

scherzo Italian for joke, a more powerful successor to the minuet, and also in triple time.

score Copy of the printed music.

septet Seven performers, or a work for seven performers.

serenade Flexible description of a work for a small group of performers, in several movements, for light-hearted entertainment.

sextet Six performers, or a work for six performers.

sonata Work for one or two performers, usually of three or four movements, with a structure within the movements.

sonata-form A structure applied to many classical compositions, particularly first movements. The movement has three sections; exposition, development and recapitulation. In the exposition, the first and second themes are stated; in the development section, the composer treats the themes in new ways; in the recapitulation he returns to the original themes.

soprano Highest female voice.

strings Violin, viola, cello, and double-bass instruments.

suite Instrumental piece in several movements.

symphony A sonata for orchestra.

Te Deum Latin hymn, 'We praise thee O God'

tempo Speed of the music.

tenor The highest natural male voice.

toccata Instrumental work generally of one fast movement.

tremolo Shimmering effect on string instruments.

triple time Rhythm that includes waltz and minuet.

variation A different treatment of a particular passage.

virtuoso An instrumentalist of outstanding technical ability.

vivace Lively.

wind instruments Instruments where the sound is created by the player's breath, and comprises the brass and woodwind.

woodwind The wind instruments historically made of wood, primarily the oboe, flute, bassoon, and clarinet.